Writing a Graduate Thesis or Dissertation

TEACHING WRITING

Volume 4

Scope

The *Teaching Writing* series publishes concise instructional writing guides. Series books each focus on a different subject area, discipline or type of writing. The books are intended to be used in undergraduate and graduate courses across the disciplines and can also be read by individual researchers or students engaged in thesis work.

Series authors must have a demonstrated publishing record and must hold a PhD, MFA or the equivalent. Please email queries to the series editor at pleavy7@aol.com

Writing a Graduate Thesis or Dissertation

Lorrie Blair
Concordia University, Canada

SENSE PUBLISHERS
ROTTERDAM/BOSTON/TAIPEI

A C.I.P. record for this book is available from the Library of Congress.

ISBN: 978-94-6300-424-4 (paperback)
ISBN: 978-94-6300-425-1 (hardback)
ISBN: 978-94-6300-426-8 (e-book)

Published by: Sense Publishers,
P.O. Box 21858,
3001 AW Rotterdam,
The Netherlands
https://www.sensepublishers.com/

All chapters in this book have undergone peer review.

Printed on acid-free paper

PRAISE FOR
WRITING A GRADUATE THESIS OR DISSERTATION

"Like a series of productive meetings with a trusted advisor, each chapter of this text provides practical information and sound insight, thoughtfully organized and generously shared. A uniquely inclusive consideration of the process of graduate research, this is the companion that graduate students crave. Attentive to the academic issues and personal trials that often accompany thesis writing in the arts, humanities, and sciences, Lorrie Blair offers a guide that is comprehensive and clear, sensitive to the distinctions among fields, and sympathetic to the various ways that the process can confuse and confound scholars in the making."
– Christine Marmé Thompson, Professor of Art Education, School of Visual Arts, Pennsylvania State University

"Dr. Lorrie Blair provides a much-needed book for students pursuing a graduate degree. *Writing a Graduate Thesis or Dissertation* is a comprehensive guide to the stages of working through the rigors of writing and defending a graduate degree from the initial stages of choosing a thesis topic and supervisor, right through to the defense of the work. Each chapter can be consulted separately, or the whole book read to give a wide-ranging understanding of the issues most pertinent to writing and defending a thesis. This book provides something for everyone involved in that process.

Both graduate students and their supervisors will find this a refreshing and thorough collection that addresses the topic across a wide range of disciplines. I wish this book had been available during my 30 years as a University Professor. With almost 100 graduate students supervised, I know that there are particular topics like plagiarism, how to conduct a literature review and ethical issues that are important for students to really understand as they begin their research and writing. The chapters on research methodology are clear and written to give access to a number of questions that students ask when trying to decide on how to conduct their research and strategies to help make their thesis a reality. This book is a highly readable, informative and welcome addition to academic literature."
– Kit Grauer, Professor Emerita, Department of Curriculum and Pedagogy, The University of British Columbia

"Dr. Lorrie Blair's complex, yet thoughtful and accessible account of the graduate research experience and thesis/dissertation writing process resonated strongly with my recent experience as a Ph.D. student. This book provides a detailed, well-structured, pragmatic guide to navigating the thresholds of graduate work, which reflects the author's many years as an extremely well respected professor, teacher, mentor and graduate supervisor. More than simply comprehensive, this work

includes information and considerations that are rarely addressed in other guides, including information related to selecting supervisors and alternative forms of research methodologies and format styles. Throughout this book, Blair weaves in a discussion of relevant contemporary challenges and affordances of academic life and professional expectations of graduate students. She discusses potential political land mines to avoid and suggests practical and insightful considerations for all levels of the thesis/dissertation process. In short, this book is a must for graduate students at any stage in their graduate career."
– Adrienne Boulton-Funke, Assistant Professor, Art and Design, Missouri State University

"Dr. Blair's writing is up-to-date, clear, and practical without being dogmatic. Her thoughtful analyses of a wide range of traditional and alternative processes prepare readers to make their own informed decisions. I highly recommend it for graduate students as well as faculty advisors."
– E. Louis Lankford, Des Lee Foundation Endowed Professor in Art Education, University of Missouri-Saint Louis

"Dr. Blair's book provides a much needed map for graduate students through the many complexities of a Ph.D. program. The chapters on supervisors are especially helpful for providing perspective on a crucial and sometimes difficult to navigate relationship. In my role providing teaching support for Teaching Assistants, I often talk to graduate students looking for perspective or help negotiating their relationship with their supervisor. I am glad I now have this book to suggest as an additional resource in these conversations."
– Shaya Golparian, Educational Developer: TA Development Programs, Centre for Teaching and Learning Development, The University of British Columbia

"When I received this book, I expected a useful generic handbook that I could refer to my graduate students. However, what I read was so much more!

Dr. Blair has produced a rich and detailed map to orient graduate students to the (oftentimes) mysterious process of successfully navigating a thesis and supervisory relationship. Her work is grounded in current knowledge about the issues dogging graduate students today, the building blocks for producing a quality thesis, and the practices and pitfalls of becoming a scholar.

But this work is also infused by the hallmark of a good supervisor. Her understanding of and caring for graduate students shines through. Her subtle wit balances out her sage advice. And most importantly, she surfaces the tacit, unspoken dimensions of graduate education: supervisors to avoid, the order of authorship, and dealing with problems in the supervisory relationship, to name just a few.

To paraphrase the Wizard of Oz: Pay attention to this woman behind the curtain."
– Rosemary C. Reilly, Associate Professor and Graduate Program Director, Applied Human Science, Concordia University

"Dr. Lorrie Blair's book is a valuable resource for every graduate student who needs to write a thesis. Filled with practical advice, this book covers the basics including differentiating between the various thesis formats, preparing the proposal, writing the literature review, choosing a methodology, collecting and analyzing data, and defending the thesis. The book also deals with the many interpersonal issues important to graduate students, including finding the right supervisor and dealing with problems that might arise between students and supervisors. The book presents sound advice regarding how to establish an academic track record by presenting research at conferences and publishing journal articles. Finally, the book is an excellent resource on the important issues of academic integrity and research ethics. For graduate students, it's common to feel overwhelmed when writing a thesis. This short volume, written in accessible language, provides graduate students with the formula for writing a successful thesis by following a series of clearly-defined steps. This will become a 'must-have' volume for every graduate student's book shelf, with advice for every step of the thesis journey."
– **Anne Lavack, Professor of Marketing, School of Business and Economics, Thompson Rivers University**

"*Writing a Graduate Thesis or Dissertation* provides a needed guide to writing a thesis or dissertation in a highly readable format. The content includes many tacit issues such as considerations for choosing a supervisor, insights into faculty rank and what they may mean for working with a supervisor, different thesis formats, the autonomy involved in writing a thesis vs. writing a class paper, and various potential roadblocks students may encounter. Readers will find this an excellent guide; I plan to incorporate it into my next graduate research course."
– **Elizabeth Garber, Professor, School of Art, The University of Arizona**

"Approaching the writing of a graduate thesis or dissertation can be a daunting task. Dr. Blair offers clearly articulated direction and nuanced detail that well assist both graduate students and their supervisors. She removes the mystique that surrounds the process, advancing ideas about how to approach decision-making and moving the research and writing forward – the right supervisor, proposal, literature review, methodology, data collection and analysis, along with building academic credentials. Questions are addressed that often graduate students fear to ask about student-supervisor problems. Enjoyment in the process is encouraged in sharp contrast to enduring a heavily straining task. The book is certainly one that I will recommend to my graduate students. Bravo for giving us a well crafted text that graduate students can use for direction and detail in the same way they utilize academic style manuals."
– **Mary Leigh Morbey, Associate Professor of Culture and Technology, Faculty of Education, York University**

This book is dedicated to Dr. Terry Barrett, my thesis supervisor, mentor, role model, and friend

TABLE OF CONTENTS

ACKNOWLEDGMENTS

I would like to acknowledge those who provided generous support for this book. Foremost, I thank Dr. Patricia Leavy for her vision and trust. Thank you, Carol Gigliotti for strengthening the manuscript. Thank you, Dr. Juan Castro, for the many insightful conversations, encouragement, and humor that enliven the pages of this book. I thank Dr. David Pariser and Larissa Yousoubova for being sounding boards and providing valuable resources.

I would like to thank all graduate students with whom I had the pleasure to work, both former and current. I have learned so much from each of you. I am especially grateful to Adrienne Alton Figliuzzi, Sebastien Fitch, and Nicole Macoretta for reading and commenting on earlier drafts. I am grateful to Seonjeong Yi for sharing her insights about the challenges faced by international students.

Thanks to those who helped me understand the diverse disciplines, especially Drs. Paula Wood-Adams, Axel van den Berg, Mary Dean, James Grant, Richard MacKenzie, and Thomas Sork. Thank you for sharing your wisdom and supervisory experiences.

Thank you, Jean-François Frappier, for your unconditional support and belief in me. I could not have written this book without you.

INTRODUCTION

This book was written to give graduate students from a variety of disciplines the tools they need to successfully research, write, and defend their thesis or dissertation. It is for those facing a blank page, having problems communicating with their supervisor, or drowning in their data. It presents frank discussions about the pitfalls and unrealistic expectations that derail thesis research and provides strategies to avoid or remedy them.

Sweeping changes in higher education are taking place in institutions around the world bringing about a fundamental restructuring of how students research and write theses (McCallin & Nayar, 2012). At the master's level, completion times are accelerated and programs that once took three years to complete now can be done in one. In many disciplines, students are "fast-tracked" into doctoral programs before writing a master's thesis. Graduate students are expected to produce high quality, innovative research and do so in decreasing amounts of time (Lee, 2007). They are expected to publish their research and apply for grants, while still students. Changes in the labor market and soaring tuition costs are, in part, driving these changes. Online programs have replaced residency requirements, allowing greater access to education and influencing how professors teach and interact with their students.

Attrition rates and time to completion rates for some disciplines have caused more than one author to refer to them as "scandals." Research indicates that many students who enter doctoral programs do not complete them (Golde, 2005). There are wide discrepancies across the disciplines. In graduate programs in education, for example, the attrition rate is estimated to be between 50–70% and time to completion as long as 12.7 years (Spaulding & Rockinson-Szapkiw, 2012). These surprisingly long completion times and attrition rates are costly and, in many cases, avoidable. Most students who dropped out later regret doing so.

Graduate research is complex and discipline specific. Students working in groups in their supervisor's lab will have very different concerns than will arts and humanities students who work independently. What works in one discipline, one program, or even with one supervisor, may not work in another situation. Supervisors can change advising styles as they progress through the academic ranks, or work differently with individual students.

Throughout this book, I use qualifiers like "in most cases," "often," and "generally" to remind readers there are always exceptions and very few rules.

To obtain a wider view of graduate school, I adopted a research method known as bricolage. Kincheloe, McLauren, and Steinberg (2011) describe the bricoleur as a "handyman or handywoman who uses all the tools available to complete a task" (p. 168). The tools I have at hand are my experiences as a supervisor, the stories others tell me about their experiences, and a wealth of recent research about thesis supervision conducted around the world. I use all these resources to provide accurate, up-to-date, and useful advice. When considering the complex world of graduate supervision, the notion of bricolage serves well because as Kincheloe et al. (2011) point out, it "exists out of respect for the complexity of the lived world and complications of power" (p. 168).

To gain a broader perspective of the graduate experience in other disciplines and universities, I sought advice from supervisors in other disciplines. My goal was to consider a number of thesis supervisory models and institutional contexts in order to represent a cross section of humanities, social sciences, natural sciences, and applied programs. Those I interviewed supervised students at both the master and doctoral levels. Most had supervised over thirty students and nearly all were enthusiastic about their roles as a supervisor.

A wealth of research has been and continues to be conducted about graduate school, and much of it seeks the voices of students and supervisors, through survey, focus groups, or interviews. I examined the existing literature, paying close attention to studies that report graduate students' and supervisors' narratives. Reading the narratives from these published studies challenged some of my long-held assumptions and reinforced others.

In addition to the resources outlined above, I give workshops on building and maintaining effective student-supervisor relationships for students at my university. Often students attending are from a wide range of disciples, but they ask similar questions. "How long should I wait for my supervisor to answer my email?" "My supervisor doesn't like me, what should I do?" Their questions inform this book. I am mindful that although I have read over one hundred theses, my reader is writing his or her first. When I told one of my students I was writing this book, he offered this advice: "...remember that often the things that we take for granted as being common knowledge not worth mentioning, aren't actually as common or as obvious as we think. In other words; include everything!" Indeed, much of the knowledge taken for granted about how to act and learn in graduate school is tacit. Without reflecting upon them, students and supervisors act out long traditions that make the academy both special and sacred. In this book, I speak openly about tacit academic knowledge.

There are many metaphors used to describe graduate school. Some refer to exams and thesis writing as hurdles to overcome. Dealing with academic regulations is like jumping through a series of hoops, some of which are on fire. I believe graduate school can, and should, be a pleasurable time in one's life, rather than an ordeal one has to endure. I adhere to a conceptual model of graduate research as a personal journey of discovery.

Although students travel similar paths, starting with compulsory courses, comprehensive exams, writing a proposal, and so on, they do not always progress in a linear fashion. Some loop back, others take diversions. Some pass though quickly, others become stuck at various points. Yet, most students deal with the same constraints of resources, time, and knowledge (Single, 2010).

OUTLINE OF CHAPTERS

Each chapter in this book represents a rite of passage common to most programs: selecting a supervisor, writing a proposal, carrying out research, analyzing data, and writing and defending a thesis. The book progresses in a linear fashion common to most graduate programs, but each chapter is independent and can be consulted as needed. To use another metaphor, most major purchases such as a car, a computer, or a toaster come with a user's manual. Some read the manual cover to cover before using their purchase. Others use the manual to troubleshoot and diagnose problems when the car won't start or the toast burns. This book is intended for both. Reading the chapters in order will help provide a smoother journey. Students will know what to expect and how to prepare. For those in the midst of their graduate journey, it offers advice on how to fix immediate problems.

Chapter 1 introduces various thesis forms and outlines the advantages and disadvantages associated with each form. Chapter 2 provides a detailed discussion about selecting a supervisor and guiding questions to help students choose mentor styles that best fit their needs. It also describes the lived experiences of professors, their academic ranks and roles, and the stress that accompanies each.

Chapter 3, the proposal, is in two parts. The first part offers students strategies to unblock and face the challenges of working independently. The second part addresses constraints students should consider when selecting a topic of research and proposing a methodology.

The literature review, Chapter 4, addresses types of reviews and offers suggestions on how to assess existing literature. Chapter 5 answers three questions student ask about plagiarism. What is it? How can it be prevented? What happens if I am charged with plagiarism? These two chapters should be read together because students are often at risk of committing plagiarism when citing literature.

The following two chapters take up the issue of research methodology. Chapter 6 provides an introduction to research methodologies and briefly describes quantitative and qualitative approaches. It includes more detailed sections about action research and arts inquiry. The chapter concludes with strategies to write a methodology section or chapter. Ethics are an integral part of the research process, and Chapter 7 details the ethical concerns involved with research using humans.

Chapter 8 addresses challenges students encounter when collecting and coding data. Once data is collected, students then must make sense of the data. This chapter offers a realistic and helpful guide to doing just that. Chapter 9 offers strategies for presenting at conferences and publishing in peer-reviewed journals. It addresses questions of authorship and intellectual property rights.

Chapter 10 is concerned with support writing the thesis and working with one's supervisor. It addresses student questions such as, how long to wait for an unanswered email, or how to prepare for a productive meeting with a supervisor. Chapter 11 offers advice for dealing with student-supervisor problems. Chapter 12 addresses the final step of graduate studies: the defense.

I hope that by reading this book, many graduate students will become better informed about the various stages in the thesis process. By knowing what to expect in each stage and how to address the demands of the process, the thesis journey should become a little less stressful and perhaps more enjoyable.

CHAPTER 1

WHAT IS A THESIS?

A completed thesis or dissertation is a major accomplishment of sustained concentration. It represents setting and achieving a high academic goal. Often the words "thesis" and "dissertation" are used interchangeably and there is no clear distinction between them. In some contexts, thesis refers to that completed at the master's level, while dissertation refers to the doctoral level. In other contexts, the opposite is true. For pragmatic purposes, I will apply the term thesis to both levels. At the most basic understanding, a thesis is the result of a substantial piece of research and scholarly writing executed with a high level of autonomy. This is the case for both master and doctoral level theses, but a doctoral thesis carries the added responsibility of presenting proof of original contribution to knowledge.

The notion of what constitutes a thesis differs greatly among disciplines. Individual programs determine the preferred format, length, and criteria of an acceptable thesis. These factors change over time and today's theses are quite different from those written as little as ten years ago (Paltridge, 2002). New methodologies have been introduced and some thesis committees now accept innovative formats. In recent years, theses have taken the form of a novel, a comic book, or a script for a play.

THESIS FORMATS

The student's field, supervisor, and program largely dictate the choice of thesis format. Some supervisors are amenable to allowing students to extend the boundaries of thesis form and methodologies, while others hold views that are more traditional. Each format has advantages and disadvantages, and the supervisor and committee should be supportive in regards to the format selected by the student.

Monographs

The standard thesis is a single, book-like monograph that contains interlinking chapters, usually an introduction, literature review, methodology, the research findings, and a conclusion clearly identifying the contribution to knowledge. Some theses conclude by indicating the need for future research and questions or directions that emerged from the research. Generally, a typical master's level thesis is not more than 150 pages and the doctoral thesis is around 300 pages. Theses as long as 600 pages do exist, but this is not recommended. It is common in the humanities and social sciences to revise the thesis into a publishable book, and a 600-page tome will require substantial reworking.

In the past, theses were bound and students were required to provide copies for the library and program. Often, they gave one as a gift to the supervisor. Today, most theses are published online, which reduces the student's costs and allows for much greater access.

The major disadvantage of monograph theses is the time they take to write. They can then be published as a book or a series of chapters, but crafting publishable papers from the thesis requires additional work. Chapters rarely conform to the word counts or form of published papers. For this reason, many programs that traditionally required monograph theses are rethinking their practices to include theses by publication.

Thesis by Publication

The thesis by publication is a collection of related papers either accepted or submitted for publication in research journals. The papers are linked by theoretical or practical connections that frame the research. The thesis can contain any number of papers, but most thesis committees require between three and seven. It is expected that the papers will have been published in peer-reviewed journals, and that the candidate is the first author or the major contributor of ideas and experimental data. In some disciplines, the first chapter must be published, the second submitted for review, and the last in progress at the time of the oral defense. Other programs expect all chapters to have been published or accepted for publication.

The thesis by publications better prepares students to take on future roles as researchers. As part of their studies, students learn to write for publication rather than complete a monograph, and then rewrite for publication. Each form requires a different set of writing skills, doubling the student's workload. This model allows for and encourages faster dissemination of research, something that is important in highly competitive fields where information and technology demand innovations. By the time a student would have written and defended a monograph thesis, the topic or research might be obsolete or published by another researcher.

The thesis by publication model responds to expectations of granting agencies that look favorably on the applicant's track record of published articles. Graduating students with strong publication records hold an advantage over others in securing post doctorate or tenure track positions. Thesis committee members and examiners are impressed or at least reassured of the quality of the overall thesis because the papers have been peer reviewed by external reviewers.

However, publishing a series of papers is no guarantee the thesis will be accepted by the supervisor or examining committee. As with all theses, it must meet the requirements of an original contribution to knowledge. Additionally, to be an accepted thesis, the papers must form a coherent document and be more than a group of single, unrelated published papers. The student must connect the individual papers through an introduction and make theoretical connections between the papers.

Publishing a paper involves a number of factors outside of a student's control. This format means the student must please members of the field, who may be less sympathetic than her or his thesis committee. Meeting the requirement of a number of publications may take considerable time. The rejection rate for top-tier journals is high and some do not allow for multiple revisions of a paper. In these cases, more time may be spent crafting a research article than actually crafting research.

At times, reviewers take months to return manuscripts to the editors. This means the paper is in limbo, neither accepted nor rejected. Students must either wait for the review or withdraw it before submitting it for consideration to another journal. Reviewers may be in disagreement over required changes or require major modifications. One reviewer may accept a paper with fairly minor modifications while another will ask for substantial changes. Usually, the editor will help negotiate these contrasting views.

Professional Doctorates

Professional doctorates embed research into the student's professional practice. Since the emphasis is on concerns related to the practice, research can be carried out within her or his own organization. This type of research is used most often in fields such as medicine, education, engineering, social work, and business. The research and thesis brings together knowledge gained from professional practice and academic theories, and students are expected to make contributions to both. In order to complete a professional doctorate, students are required to carry out research but the professional doctorate thesis can take many forms, including a monograph, a portfolio, or a series of published reports (Wellington & Sikes, 2006). Publications may be single authored or collaborative reports, depending on the regulations of each university or department.

The advantage of the professional doctorate is that research compliments the student's working life (Fenge, 2009). The research is likely to be personally meaningful, which encourages completion rates. The main disadvantages associated with professional doctorates are that conflicts of interest and ethical tensions may arise during the research and writing process. For those with professional experience, occupying the role of a student blurs the normal boundaries of both the work and academic environment. Fulfilling the requirements of both roles may take a particular level of sensitivity. In addition, as a researcher, students may be hesitant to reveal findings that show their organization in a bad light. Revealing these findings can have a negative and lasting impact on the student's professional career that continues beyond the thesis defense. However, the professional doctorate can provide a real world application to research and bridge the theory/practice divide.

Thesis and a Creative Project

The Master of Fine Arts (MFA) was long considered to be a terminal degree for artists and writers. Usually, those teaching and working in arts related fields, such as literature, creative writing, theatre, museology, and media arts, did not pursue a doctorate in art, nor were they required to hold the degree to obtain a teaching position in art schools (Milech & Schilo, 2009). Those who wished to continue their studies enrolled in programs leading to a Ph.D. However, as the arts entered universities, faculties and granting agencies began to debate what constituted creative research. Scholars began to ask what a production-based doctoral thesis might entail. There are lively, and ongoing debates about the format, goals, and purpose of the written component that accompanies a body of art.

In Australia, and some other countries, the written component of a production-based thesis is referred to as an "exegesis." There are three widely used exegesis models: the context model, the commentary model, and the research question model (Milech & Schilo, 2009). The context model is the most traditional of the three, and requires students first to create a cohesive body of artwork, and then write a document that contextualizes and situates it within the larger art world. According to Milech and Schilo, the thesis "rehearses the historical, social and/or disciplinary context(s) within which the student developed the creative or production component of her or his thesis" (p. 6). Creation is viewed as the practice whereas the written component is considered to be the accompanying theory. The commentary model describes the process the student went through to create the work, and retains the theory/practice divide (Milech & Schilo, 2009). The research question model explores the same question independently through production and a written component, with each component using a different language to answer the single question. Together, the two parts form a cohesive whole. While I agree with the premise and merit of this model, I believe it requires an undue amount of work, requiring an artist/scholar to be the master of two languages. It denies the power of artwork or creative effort to stand on its own. I am not alone in my questions about the goals and use of the exegesis. Bourke and Neilsen (2004) note that students question whether they should be required to validate their creative work through writing. Those who advocate for alternative and art-based theses take up this issue.

Alternative Forms

At the 1996 American Educational Research Association conference, Howard Gardner and Elliott Eisner, both leaders in education research, debated the question, "Should novels count as doctoral dissertations in education?" (Donmoyer, Eisner, & Gardner, 1996). Eisner, arguing for the affirmative, won the debate and by 1999, the first novel as dissertation appeared (Dunlop, 1999). North American educators began to theorize about arts-based research, resulting in a proliferation of books advocating for this method (Barone & Eisner, 2012; Leavy, 2015). Comics, films, plays, and a variety of other forms have now been accepted as theses.

Biklen and Casella (2007) end their book, *A Practical Guide to the Qualitative Dissertation*, with a caveat to students considering writing what they call a non-traditional thesis. They warn that a non-traditional thesis demands more of a student than does one written in the tradition of the discipline, and students who choose to take on this endeavor make an already challenging task more difficult. Students who, for example, choose to write a novel must know their research well. Additionally, they must know the conventions of the novel form, and they must be able to write their research findings in that convention. Similarly, Kamler and Thompson (2006) warn, "Bad poetry does not achieve the goals of either enhanced meaning making or a successful representation of a scholar on top of their material" (p. 143). Biklen and Casella also suggest that producing a non-traditional thesis can affect the student's future career. They warn this kind of thesis may lower one's chances of employment because these theses may be viewed as suspect and unscholarly.

At issue for Kamler and Thompson, I believe, is that art is a subjective form and in our postmodern times, it is difficult to judge the quality of art. Moreover, their statement implies that students write bad poetry. It is possible a student will write good poetry and perhaps good poetry can achieve more than would a standard thesis. Barone and Eisner (2012) note that the arts have the capacity to reach a wider audience than does traditional academic writing. While I agree with Biklen and Casella that writing or drawing the non-traditional thesis can be more challenging and more time consuming than a traditional one, there may be good reason to take on the additional challenge. I recently supervised a master's level student whose thesis explored the pedagogical capacity of drawing comics. Her thesis was presented in a comic book format. Jacob (2014) wrote her thesis in a traditional manner, and then reworked the data into a comic book. The comic added an additional layer over the text, increasing the reader's understanding. However, I remarked to her that if she had simply written the thesis, she would have completed it six months faster. She replied, "Yes, but I wouldn't have loved it."

Most universities now make theses available online, affording students the opportunity to peruse theses written by former students in their department, as well as those from graduates of universities around the world. Taking time to examine other theses provides students with an idea of what topics and methodologies are current in the field. Students can also note writing tone and structure used in their discipline. In choosing a thesis format, it is wise to have supervisor support. Additionally, considering the time they wish to spend crafting a thesis and reflecting on their goals for the future are both important elements in choosing a thesis format. Innovative formats require more time than the tradition theses, but students may wish to take on this challenge. Students may not love their thesis, but writing it should be a pleasurable experience.

CHAPTER 2

FINDING THE RIGHT SUPERVISOR

INTRODUCTION

The process of writing a thesis begins long before one sits down to put words on paper. It begins with the choice of what to study, where to study, and most importantly, with whom to study. Although graduate students interact with many professors, their primary relationship is with their supervisor, and this relationship plays a major factor in their success or failure during their studies and beyond earning the degree. Even if readers are already enrolled in a graduate program, this chapter provides the departmental and institutional context in which the supervisory relationship takes place. For students still searching for a supervisor, this chapter provides some strategies and guiding questions to help them make their decision.

Programs have customized approaches to selecting a supervisor. Some programs require incoming students to secure a faculty member who will commit to act as a supervisor for their research. In many of these cases, the supervisor provides them with full or partial funding. Other programs accept students and allow them a grace period to find a supervisor. In these cases, admittance is conditional and students who cannot persuade a faculty member to supervise their research are withdrawn from the program. The time allowed for this can vary from two months to several years. Other programs assign all admitted students to a supervisor. The rules and procedures for selecting a supervisor may be found in program descriptions, but this information might not be evident in their application procedures. Many universities have institutional guidelines for students, faculty, and administration. Usually, these guidelines are available from the university's school of graduate studies and most are posted online. Graduate Program Directors (GPDs) can provide specific program guidelines concerning the procedures surrounding supervisor selection.

David Mumby (2012), author of *Graduate School: Winning Strategies for Getting In*, notes that the choice of a supervisor should supersede the choice of a university. This is excellent advice in that graduate research is closely linked to a specific researcher, not an institution. However, not all students are in this ideal situation. Students are not always admitted to their first choice university or program. For others, personal reasons, such as family responsibilities and financial constraints, limit their choice of where to study. Many cannot leave jobs and instead elect to study part-time at a university near their home. Master's level students, when compared to doctoral students, have less pressure to "get it right," simply due to length of their programs. Typically, a master's level student will spend only one or two years working directly with their supervisor, whereas a doctoral student may spend from four to seven years.

Even for programs that do not require a supervisor for admittance, having a supervisor might increase a student's chance of being admitted because it is likely that the faculty member may speak favorably about them during the admission process. Additionally, securing an advisor early gives students a better chance of selecting their preferred supervisor. On the other hand, students might meet another faculty member with whom they would prefer to work. Changing supervisors is not a simple matter and, in some cases, doing so can have negative consequences. This point will be taken up in greater detail in Chapter 11.

Most universities and programs use a traditional model of supervision that involves a close working relationship between a student and one faculty member. The supervisor guides the research and serves as a mentor for the duration of the degree. Effective supervisors do more than help students write their thesis. They serve as role models who socialize students and help them understand and adopt the discipline's values, methods, and ways of constructing knowledge (Fanghanel, 2009). Successful selection means aligning one's research interests, goals for study, and ways of working with the potential supervisor. The traditional model is well suited for self-directed students who are well prepared for graduate work.

Other programs use a blended approach that augments one-on-one supervisory sessions with group meetings and writing groups. Programs where students work in labs on common problems, such as in science and engineering, most often use the blended approach. Some programs are oriented toward the professional doctorate in which research is carried out in the place of employment and collaborative essays may replace the single authored monograph theses (Lee, 2007).

Who Are Supervisors?

In most universities, supervision is a voluntary activity for faculty members. Faculty members are expected, but not required to work with graduate students. Moreover, students do not always get the supervisor they want. Busy and popular supervisors may not accept additional students, and it is common for supervisors to limit the number of students with whom they work. Supervisors know how many students their labs can accommodate and for how many they can provide adequate funding. Generally speaking, no supervisor is forced to work with a specific student, and in most cases, a student is not required to work with a particular supervisor. However, there are programs that assign supervisors to incoming students based on their area of research interest. This assignment method ensures that faculty members share the workload and supervision is balanced. This also means some students will work with their preferred supervisor, while others may not.

In most universities, only full-time faculty members are permitted to supervise graduate students. Others, such as part-time instructors, adjunct professors, and Limited Term instructors are contractual employees. Their employment usually is dependent on a number of factors, such as the current sabbatical or leave replacements needed and course enrollment. Full-time faculty members, on the other hand, have permanent positions and are likely to be employed for the duration of a student's program, a plus for students who are happy with their supervisor.

Student Needs

Before turning attention to finding the right supervisor, it is necessary to consider what students want and need from this relationship. Tenenbaum, Crosby, and Gliner (2001) surveyed students at their California university and found three types of help students expect to receive ideally from their supervisors: psychosocial, instrumental, and networking. To their list, I would add the need for financial aid. For Tenenbaum et al. (2001) supervisors meet their students' psychosocial needs when they convey empathy for their concerns and feelings. These supervisors allow and encourage students to discuss concerns regarding feelings they have about their competencies and academic abilities. They encourage students to talk openly about personal anxieties and fears that deter them from working and are open to sharing their own personal stories about how they overcame similar obstacles. In a narrative describing her doctoral work, Lakkala (2012) illustrates how her supervisor provided psychosocial help. She writes,

> She paid attention to my feelings when she had to give feedback that demanded changes ... She discretely anticipated the emotional reactions the various phases would cause. Along with the process, I had to learn

that my feelings of incapability and being wounded were inevitable. (p. 14)

Supervisors provide instrumental help when they give assistance to improve students' writing skills, help them organize and deliver a conference presentation, and explore their career options. Supervisors can help their students find the right venue for publications, and mentor them on how to write and submit a paper for publication. Networking help involves introducing students to other researchers in the field. It may also mean writing letters of reference for jobs and grants. Supervisors can advocate for students in departmental decisions about teaching and research assistantships, and provide other means of financial support. Many pay travel expenses, which permits their students to attend conferences and network with other researchers.

Asking themselves what they most want and need from a supervisor and then identifying the faculty member who is best is suited to meet those needs will prevent future disappointments with a mismatched supervisor. For example, students need to understand which is most important to them: personal supportiveness or professional competence. This is not to say that the supportive supervisor is not or cannot be an expert in her or his field, or conversely, that the professionally competent supervisor is not supportive. Being a top researcher, however, takes concentrated time and the rewards usually involve travel to attend conferences and keynote speaking engagements. It takes focus to conduct research and a supervisor's time is finite. Students who need a great deal of psychosocial support should not choose supervisors who are best suited to offer networking support. Instead, students who are highly motivated to publish and present work, and who hope to get a university position, are best mentored by active researchers.

Ideally, most supervisors would possess the skills needed to meet all three needs, but research and personal experience indicate that supervisors usually excel in one of the three areas. Some do not see it as their responsibility to support students emotionally as well as academically. James and Baldwin (1999) warn that taking on the role of a counselor is "exhausting and dangerous" (p. 34). They hold that supervisors and students should maintain a professional relationship. Students need to be clear about their expectations and supervision needs. Some students need and want a close relationship with their supervisor. Others prefer to work autonomously.

Students who attend universities in cultures or countries different from their own have greater needs than their fellow students. This is particularly the case for students who must write a thesis in a second language. These students may need more instrumental help with writing, particularly with critical analysis and argument construction. Conventions of academic scholarship may differ from their previous degrees in their own country. There may be vast differences in notions of what it means to be a good student. Those in this situation are less likely to know how to navigate university structures and may find that being a student in the new environment is quite different from that with which they are familiar. They may hold assumptions about student and teacher roles that are in contrast with the new learning environment (Zhou, Jindal-Snape, Topping, & Todman, 2008). For example, students attending North American universities from other continents may be surprised to find that they are expected to actively engage in dialogue during class, rather than simply attend lectures. Many of these students pay high tuition and fees, and feel intense pressure to succeed. Additionally, students away from home are likely to feel isolated and lack social networks. Many turn to their supervisor as their sole means of support.

Qualities to Look for in a Supervisor

Respect for a supervisor as an authority on the subject and as a leading researcher in the field will go a long way when being asked to revise a draft for the fifth time. Those I interviewed held differing opinions on how much of a domain expert the supervisor should be and answers ranged from "possessing a passing knowledge" to "the leading expert in the field." Ideally, the supervisor should be knowledgeable about either the topic or research methodology the student intends to explore in his or her thesis. Supervisors with domain knowledge can direct their students to the most pertinent literature and current research. However, the match between the student's needs and the supervisor's ability and willingness to meet those needs may be more important than subject expertise.

The research topic is only one factor that should influence who students select as a supervisor. They must be comfortable with the supervisor's interpersonal skills. For example, students who need positive feedback for motivation should not ask a highly critical professor to supervise. This professor is best suited to supervise students who thrive on having their ideas challenged.

THE INSTITUTIONAL CONTEXT OF SUPERVISION

Throughout their academic careers, faculty members have different responsibilities that often correspond to the rank they hold. Their time is divided between teaching, research, and service, and pressure to meet the demands of their rank greatly affects how and why they work with graduate students. Understanding the institutional context can make students aware of competing priorities, but they should note that these descriptions are generalizations. Professors at each level are individuals and approach their faculty responsibilities and supervisory roles in unique ways. In the North American context, tenure track or tenure stream professors are designated by the rank of assistant professor, associate professor, or full professor.

Assistant professors are newly hired into tenure track or tenure stream positions. They are most likely to have recently completed their doctoral or post-doctoral work. Many are teaching for the first time in their academic career. Assistant professors are given a probationary period, usually around five or six years, to prepare for consideration to be promoted to the associate level. To be promoted, assistant professors must show evidence of successful teaching and research. Evidence of research includes successful grants, peer-reviewed papers, and sometimes, books.

Tenure procedures vary among universities, but most involve a peer review process. At the end of the probationary period, assistant professors prepare a performance dossier, which will be read and assessed by a number of committees, usually starting at the program level. Those who are not awarded tenure usually leave the university. It cannot be understated how stressful the tenure process is for faculty members. Assistant professors are sometimes referred to as "junior faculty" and feel scrutinized at every turn. Adding to their stress, many assistant professors have young children and other family obligations that compete for their time.

As supervisors, assistant professors are likely to be current with research being done in their field and might be more accepting of originality and innovation. They are in a good position to help students select a relevant and timely research topic. This is particularly the case in fields driven by innovation and where technology is always in a state of flux. Assistant professors are often funded by university start-up grants and government grants specifically targeted for new professors. They are highly motivated to publish and are likely to encourage students to publish with them. Supervising master's students is sometimes required to achieve tenure. At the very least, tenure committees look upon supervision favorably, and success is measured by the completion rates of their students.

During the first few years in the tenure track position, the assistant professor will likely have very little experience in supervising students. They are only a few years from their own graduate work, and research shows that the supervisor's previous experience as a doctoral student is a key influence on how they, in turn, supervise (Delamont, Parry, & Atkinson, 1998; Lee, 2007). They may have unrealistic expectations for the students they supervise or be disappointed when their students do not possess the same skill level or work ethic they believe themselves to have had as a student.

Some assistant professors may be unfamiliar with their program's supervisory cultures and university policies. This may be a disadvantage in that they may be unable to help their students navigate complicated university administrative structures. However, starting fresh can be an advantage in that they may be optimistic and may consider new approaches to supervision. The biggest disadvantage to working with an assistant professor is that they are busy, and in some cases may place their own academic success over that of the students they supervise. In a worst-case scenario, the assistant professor will not receive tenure, and the graduate students he or she supervises will have to find another supervisor.

Associate Professors are usually tenured and may hold this rank either for their entire career or until they are promoted to full professor. Most associate professors are well established in their universities and field of research. Publishing and presenting papers are still important for promotion to full professor and to garner competitive research funding. As one professor recounted about tenure, "Tenure is like winning a pie eating contest and the prize is more pie."[1] Associate professors are usually expected to provide graduate student support and publication success is a condition for securing additional research grants. Scientists need money for labs, and those who are not successful in garnering grants and contracts are assigned extra teaching duties, or are assigned to teach large lectures at the undergraduate level. In some universities, associate professors are eligible for six month or yearlong sabbaticals. A sabbatical may mean students will rarely see the supervisor, and may not receive feedback.

Once tenure has been attained, the pressure to publish and apply for research grants may be less than for the assistant professor. As a result, they may have less funding to provide for their graduate students. On the other hand, they are in a good position to help students navigate university structures and have more time to devote to them.

Professors refer to all faculty members who teach courses, but not all hold the rank of a full professor. In this case, the title is used as one would use that of "teacher." Only those who demonstrate sustained quality teaching and research over a period of years may be promoted to the rank of professor. Sometimes they are referred to as full professors. To achieve this rank, those

13

at the associate level go through a peer-review process similar to tenure at the assistant professor level. In many cases, professors outside of the university evaluate their dossier.

At their best, professors have supervised many graduate students, and importantly, remain active researchers. However, stereotypes of the curmudgeon and absent-minded professor abound. In some cases some professors may be less current in their fields and their network of colleagues may be older and retired. This may be detrimental to their students' ability to network and gain future employment and they may be less open to innovative methodologies and ideas. With less expectation to publish, and even less incentive to do so, the demands on their time may be less. In addition, if they have children, they are most likely grown, and as a consequence may have more time to devote to their students' academic and psychosocial needs.

Cultural Diversity

In addition to the rank, communication style, expertise, and ability to provide help, other issues such as gender, race, ethnicity, sexual orientation, and age can affect the student-supervisor relationship. Since the 1990s, a great deal of research has been conducted about gender and graduate studies. This research was generated, in part, in response to statistics that show that women are more likely than men to drop out of graduate school, to take more time to complete, and are less likely to obtain a research position after graduation (Spaulding & Rockinson-Szapkiw, 2012). Since research indicated that the relationship between the student and supervisor was key to a student's completion, researchers turned their attention to the impact of same-gender and cross-gender supervision. In an extensive literature review, Smeby (2000) found evidence both for and against same-gender student and supervisor relationships. Some studies suggest that female students are more satisfied with female supervisors because the supervisors understand the issues that concern female students. Chapman and Sork (2001) support this notion and write that female students who have male supervisors do not have "the same opportunity to 'bond' over a beer or at a hockey game" (p. 101). They hold that female students are not afforded the same opportunities to have close personal relationships with male supervisors, as would a male student. This suggests a certain (acknowledged) stereotype that may not be the case. It infers that as a female, I would enjoy shopping with my students, which I do not, and that I do not watch hockey and drink beer, which I do.

As a mother, I am aware of the difficulties women face when trying to write a thesis and at the same time, manage a young child. However, my colleague, a sleep-deprived father of two toddlers, may have greater insight.

Research indicates that female supervisors provide more psychosocial help to female students than to male students and that male supervisors provide less psychosocial help than their female counterparts. (Tenenbaum, Crosby, & Gliner, 2001). They found that male students published more with their supervisors than did women across all disciplines. Other studies suggest that supervisor's gender makes little difference because senior female faculty members gained entrance into the academy and thrived there because they share the same values as their male counterparts (Smeby, 2000).

For Chapman and Sork (2001), the issue is not simply the lack of buddy relationship, but that these relationships bring with them access to power. This is a problem in the life sciences where studies show women are provided less funding, given less access to elite laboratories, and that women with children are less likely to be hired for tenure track positions than men with children (Sheltzer & Smith, 2014). Women are underrepresented in prestigious laboratories. Sheltzer and Smith found that elite male faculty employ fewer female graduate students, but found no comparable gender bias in elite labs supervised by female scientists. However, with fewer women receiving the faculty positions there are fewer opportunities for female graduate students to have female supervisors.

This same vicious cycle is reflected in discussions about how race impacts student-supervisory relationships. It is a well documented fact that faculty of color are vastly underrepresented in most programs (Felder & Barker, 2013; Felder, Stevenson, & Gasman, 2014). This paucity of diversity means students have few choices of supervisors. Students of color report racial discrimination and perceive the exclusion in the life of a department (Felder & Barker, 2013). Doctoral students of color note that faculty inaccessibility is a barrier to forming meaningful and effective connections with the faculty (Felder & Barker, 2013). They receive less research and teaching assistantships than their white counterparts (Felder et al., 2014). Some students report faculty members do not support their research when it involves racial or cultural topics. Perhaps the faculty member had no background in understanding of the work, or as reported by Felder et al., there was an "endemic departmental insensitivity and racial stereotyping" (p. 36). Having same race peers and faculty as support is important.

It is clear there is a systemic problem that prevents faculty diversity, starting with faculty discriminating against perspective students. Milkman, Akinola, and Chugh (2013) conducted an experiment to determine if gender and racial bias started before students were admitted to graduate programs. Their study involved 6500 randomly selected professors from 258 institutions in 89 disciplines across the United States. The researchers sent each professor an email request from a fictional prospective student for an informal meeting to discuss their doctoral program. All emails were identical except for the student's name, which was validated to signal gender and race (p. 5). They found that professors were more likely to respond to Caucasian males than to women and students of color. Asian students experienced the most bias, with Asian women experiencing the worst discrimination. Discrimination is more extreme in higher paying disciplines and in private institutions. Business disciplines exhibited the most bias, whereas Fine Arts exhibited a reverse bias. Milkman et al. (2013) found that perceived minority students received a better response from professors from the same background.

The emergence of the professional doctorate degree has highlighted how age may impact the supervision relationship (Malfroy, 2005). Students who return to graduate study after extensive professional careers may find it difficult to work with a younger supervisor who has less field experience, even when the supervisor is deemed to be an expert in their field. These students may sense that theory and practice are disconnected and may rely on their own experience to argue points. Malfroy, in her ethnographic study of a research centre that focused on environmental health, management and tourism, found that some of the 11 doctoral students who were assigned there reported feeling awkward about their status as students in contrast to their status in their work place. According to Malfroy, these professionals are "having a profound impact in altering traditional hierarchal models of expert/novice" (p. 166).

Clearly, gender, race, sexual orientation, culture, religion, age, and a host of other factors affect the student-supervisory relationship, and the ideal supervisor may not exist. Before selecting a supervisor, it is vital to know that they are supportive of students and respect them. Is the supervisor open and interested to learn about their students' cultures and values? Or does the potential supervisor appear to be sexist, racist, homophobic, or otherwise unethical? The student-supervisor relationship is long-term and intense, and often lasts beyond the completion of the degree. It is worth taking the time to find the right supervisor.

FINDING THE "JUST RIGHT" SUPERVISOR

Students applying a focused approach are utilizing an essential tool for being admitted to the program of their choice. A well-crafted letter introduces the writer and demonstrates that she or he is familiar with the potential supervisor's research. This familiarity goes beyond the key words listed on websites or articles. The writer must also demonstrate, and not simply state, that there is a clear match in research interests. They need to do their homework by searching out and reading many publications by the professor. An extensive literature search can provide information about a potential supervisor's research topic and research methods. It is not a good idea to rely solely on a program's websites for accurate information because faculty profiles are notoriously out of date and incomplete. Some of the busiest professors do not update their profile.

Letters should be formal and accurately address the professor by his or her title. The title of "Dr." is preferred, if the person indeed holds a doctorate degree. "Professor" is used for those holding terminal degrees, such as MFAs. Letters must be free of typos and grammatical errors. This is especially the case concerning the professor's name. Pay particular attention to details, such as capitalization and spelling. For example, the well-known American educator, feminist, and author bell hooks should never be addressed as Bell Hooks.

If at all possible, establish a relationship with a potential supervisor before committing to a program of research. This relationship can start with a letter of introduction from a current professor, or a request to visit the school. For students seeking a master's degree, professors who teach undergraduate courses can provide suggestions of leading programs and researchers in their field. Potential doctoral students who are seeking a new direction or wish to relocate may rely on their Master's thesis supervisor for advice. Their current supervisor may be active in the field and can suggest some colleagues with whom the student might work.

Research conferences are good places to make contact with a potential supervisor. However, graduate students flock to popular researchers like groupies to a rock star. At the end of a presentation, students rush to the podium and surround the professor. It is best to contact the professor in writing before a conference, introduce yourself, and ask for a brief appointment at the professor's convenience during the conference. The best idea is to visit the campus and meet with several faculty members. Many programs hold annual graduate symposia, which would provide opportunities to meet students enrolled in the program, as well as many faculty members. If travel to the university is too costly, at least potential students should attempt a meeting through videoconferencing.

Students who are admitted to programs before selecting a supervisor have many advantages over those who must have a supervisor before being admitted. The ideal situation allows students to take courses with several faculty members. Here, students can learn a great deal by noting how professors interact with all students, how long they take to give feedback and the nature of the feedback.

For students who are already in programs and seeking supervisors, a commonly offered recommendation is to ask other students' advice. Collectively, students know a great deal about the supervisors in their program. Each student may know something, and together they can paint an accurate picture of a supervisor's style. Fellow students can provide valuable information if asked the right questions. When asking another student about his or her supervisor, first ask yourself, "Am I like this person?" Students' needs differ. A good question is not, "Do you like this professor?" but rather, "Do you like working with him or her?" This is vitally important for students who will work for extended periods in labs along side their professors and other students supervised by the professor. In particular, doctoral students who completed their Master's degree at the same institution are valuable resources. Asking if they remained with their same supervisor is helpful. If not, ask why they changed.

It should be noted that when students seek advice in this fashion, they are usually limited to speaking to the more successful students. Students, who have quit out of discouragement and exasperation are not likely to be found on campus. It is useful to take note of which professors are busy. Students, it is said, vote with their feet, and are likely to avoid undesirable supervisors. To use another metaphor, an empty restaurant is likely to either serve bad food or offer poor service. On the other hand, high profile researchers who are in demand as supervisors may not be able to provide their students with personal attention. A GPD may be able to provide information about how many students a potential supervisor is carrying, how this compares to other supervisors in the same program, and how long it takes students to graduate under his or her tutelage.

For additional information, students can read theses of other graduate students supervised by the potential supervisor. Nearly all universities require graduating students to post their theses online. If at all possible, search the literature to see how many of the supervisor's master students later went on to Ph.D. programs, noting if they continued at the same university, and if so, whether or not they continued to work with the same professor.

Supervisors to Avoid

When I asked my colleagues what kind of supervisor students should avoid, they consistently mentioned the unavailable faculty member. According to them, these professors are interested only in their own careers and their projects. They do not take the time or see it as their responsibility to mentor students. One colleague noted that these supervisors make students "data slaves" and "jerk students from project to project." However, no one I interviewed could tell me how a student would know who to avoid. Program politics are well known among faculty, but not publicly discussed. Mumby (2012) suggests asking advice from graduate program directors, but they are members of the program and may not be willing to speak badly of their colleagues.

In order to know if the faculty member is available to help the students he or she supervises, one needs to consider what "available" means to all concerned. Do students work well on their own, or do they need to see their supervisor 15 times a day? Does the supervisor see it as his or her responsibility to ensure that students work consistently and meet deadlines? Or, does the supervisor expect graduate students to work independently? Is timely feedback provided on drafts? Will the supervisor read drafts of presentations and papers for publication? Are opportunities provided for their students to co-publish or co-present? Partnerships between students and their supervisors work best when there is a match between the student's expectations and the professor's supervisory style.

Co-Supervision

Students who choose an assistant professor as their supervisor are advised to ask a more established professor to co-supervise. Some programs require compulsory co-supervision for inexperienced supervisors to ensure a common supervision culture is maintained. Some require students to name a secondary supervisor for continuity should the primary supervisor not be able to see the student to completion. Not all programs recognize co-supervision and require that only one faculty member serves as the primary supervisor. At the very least, having two professors supervise research ensures the student will have someone familiar with his or her work in place in the event the assistant professor be denied tenure or takes a maternity or paternity leave.

It is important to establish a working relationship with both supervisors and a clear agreement on how to proceed. Otherwise, one has two supervisors to satisfy. Both may read and offer feedback of drafts, but the feedback may not be consistent between the advisors. Progress may be delayed because it may take twice as long to get feedback because each reads the thesis independently, and then must find time to meet to compare notes. It is possible neither will provide feedback, thinking the other has done so. They may have competing ideas about research methods or topics, and the student is placed in an unfortunate position of having to choose the direction. Co-supervision works best when supervisors have a track record of working together. Before committing to co-supervision, note how many times the two professors have supervised together. If professors in the program frequently co-supervise, this usually means the above issues most likely have been resolved.

The Thesis Committee

In addition to having a primary supervisor, many programs also require students to have an advisory committee. This usually consists of the supervisor and two or three other members. The other members can be from the same program or from other related programs. In some cases, faculty members from other universities may be invited to sit on thesis committees. Forming a committee should be done in consultation with one's supervisor. Supervisors will suggest people with whom they have worked in the past and who hold similar ideas about thesis research. Supervisory groups can remedy certain problems inherent in the close student and supervisor relationship, but that they can also create problems. Committee members do not always agree on the direction research should take or provide consistent assessment of the thesis. It is important that supervisors be able to advocate for their students. Untenured faculty members may be hesitant to disagree with a senior member who is in a position to vote against their tenure.

It is important to learn program protocol concerning how committees function. In some cases, all research is carried out with the supervisor and the committee serves as the examining committee. In other cases, students can consult committee members throughout the research process. When asking faculty members to serve on the committee, consider what expertise or role will be expected from them. What do they bring to the topic or research methodology? It is important to meet with and discuss research interests with potential committee members. Time is a professor's most valuable commodity so ensure that it is not wasted. One professor I interviewed spoke of meeting with a student, but not receiving any follow up correspondence. This professor was surprised to find herself summoned to a committee meeting, and as a result, declined to serve. Another was under the impression he was serving on committee only to discover some time later that another colleague had replaced him. If after meeting, it is determined this professor is not a good fit for the committee, be polite, and send a thank you letter. In some cases, committee members must excuse themselves, and students may need to find replacements. In other words, avoid burning bridges. The first thing the committee will review is your thesis proposal. The next chapter focuses on this essential piece of your thesis plan.

NOTE

[1] This is a quote from the twitter site, Shit Academics Say. The quote is "Academic life is less like a box of chocolate and more like a pie eating contest where the prize is more pie." https://twitter.com/academicssay/status/542416581561573378

WRITING THE PROPOSAL

INTRODUCTION

Thesis research starts with a clearly articulated plan of action. The better the plan, the better the thesis and the fewer problems students face as the research process unfolds. A proposal provides a detailed description of the study and assures a thesis committee that students are capable of carrying out high quality research. It demonstrates that they understand and have thought through the research process. Importantly, the proposal is a justification for the topic and methodology, and, once accepted, is a written agreement between students and their thesis committee. This chapter considers the barriers students encounter at the proposal stage and suggests practical solutions to overcome them. It provides tips on selecting a topic of research and concludes by outlining components of thesis proposals.

Practices vary as to when students are expected to write their proposal. Some programs require students to first complete a number of courses and pass a comprehensive exam before writing a proposal. For others, the research question may be established early in the program. When students work in teams to conduct research in a supervisor's lab, the supervisor may assign or suggests areas of related research for each student to carry out independently. Generally, programs in the social sciences, arts, and humanities place more responsibility and freedom on the student. Students in these programs may be expected to initiate their topic, select the theoretical perspective, and determine the appropriate methodology. This work is usually done in consultation with a supervisor.

Proposals are discipline specific and the chosen methodology frequently determines the proposal's content. For example, a proposal to test a hypothesis will differ from one that proposes a field study. However, all proposals demonstrate that the student has identified a topic of research, has read to ascertain what others have found about the topic, formulated a research question, and selected an appropriate methodology to answer that question. There is no consensus on the length or format of a proposal. They can range from two or three page outlines to the first three chapters of the thesis.

For some students, writing a thesis proposal is more difficult than writing a thesis; many who did exceptionally well in their courses flounder at the proposal stage. Students who cannot successfully master a proposal stay in an academic limbo and some drop out of their program. Gardner (2008) interviewed faculty members from departments with low completion rates at one university and found that professors attributed a "lack of focus, motivation and initiative" as the reasons doctoral students drop out of their studies (p. 103). They specifically noted that the unsuccessful student was not able to find a research question.

Personal experience and interviews with other supervisors helped me identify some of the obstacles students face during the proposal stage of research. Students must learn to manage fear and work independently. They must identify a topic that is both of interest to themselves and relevant to their field of study. In addition, they must ask a question that is both big enough to matter to a thesis committee and small enough to answer given the student's resources. In the following section, I will elaborate on each obstacle and offer strategies to overcome it.

Overcoming Fear

Some who have successfully written numerous course assignments, with little or no difficulty, panic at the thought of writing a thesis. Their fear is the result of an overwhelming, and often unrealistic, conception of what a thesis entails. Lee (2007) holds that all graduate students confront the same problem. "They ask themselves: can they ever reach the impossible standard of scholarly rigor which appears to be demanded" (p. 681).

The "imposter syndrome" is at the heart of most student fear. Described by Clance and Imes (1978), imposter syndrome was first attributed to women, who despite their outstanding academic and professional accomplishments believed they were not smart and had fooled anyone who thought otherwise. The syndrome is now regarded as a major trait among graduate students. Many graduate students fear they do not have what it takes to complete a graduate degree and are afraid others may find out. They silently worry that they are academic frauds. For some, this fear of failure and lack of self-confidence can be debilitating.

Sakulku and Alexander (2011) describe how the imposter cycle begins and is maintained. They posit that the cycle starts when a task is assigned. The task is met with anxiety, self-doubt, and fear of failure. Individuals react to the fear either by procrastinating or going into a frenzy of over preparedness. This is problematic when the amount of energy put toward accomplishing a task is excessive or interferes with other priorities. Once the task has been completed, there is a feeling of relief and accomplishment. However, this feeling is short-lived. Any positive feedback received is discounted as luck for students who procrastinate, while those who over prepare attribute it to hard work. In either case, success is not internalized or attributed to ability, intelligence, or skill level. For Clance and Imes (1978), the successful completion of a task serves to reinforce the feeling of being fraudulent, rather than diminish the fear.

The imposter syndrome is manifested at the proposal stage when students either procrastinate to write it or work to make it perfect. These students are reluctant to submit the proposal to their supervisor in fear that the supervisor will discover they are not smart enough to carry out research independently. The proposal must be perfect or nothing at all. They have no deadlines to meet, so weeks turn into semesters, and semesters into years.

I suspect that most people in academia feel like frauds, except for the real imposters and egomaniacs. One way to break the imposter cycle is to talk about it or seek counseling. Another way to break the cycle is to acknowledge the role perfectionism plays in preventing students from accomplishing their goals. Sakulku and Alexander (2011) contend that, "Perfectionism is a trait that is believed to have a marked impact on the development and maintenance of imposter fears" (p. 84). These individuals set impossibly high standards for themselves. They believe the work they submit must be flawless. All students want to do well and to be recognized as a top student, but trying to attain perfectionism has its price. It is the enemy of the graduate student. It can rob them of their time, their family and friends, and their health.

Adopting a "good enough" approach to research and academic work can help break the imposter syndrome cycle. Luttrell (2000) borrowed from child psychoanalyst D. W. Winnicott's notion of good enough mothering, since the perfect mother is a fantasy that can damage healthy relations. Luttrell's notion of being a good enough researcher helps students avoid the fantasy of the perfect student and instead encourages them to accept that mistakes are a healthy and necessary part of learning. Single (2010), author of *Demystifying Dissertation Writing*, aptly advises students to avoid overglorifying the thesis project. She writes, "Your dissertation should be the worst piece of research that you ever write—not that your dissertation should be bad, but all of your subsequent research and scholarship should be better" (p. 21).

Working Independently

Most graduate students were successful undergraduates, and for the first year of graduate studies, their program looks and feels familiar. Professors supply reading lists and clearly defined assignments to guide learning. Fellow students in the course make up a community of learners. Professors hold regular office hours and provide feedback at midterm and at the end of the course. However, an unfamiliar obstacle may be encountered when students are expected to work on a proposal with little or no guidance. Left on their own, without a peer group and imposed deadlines, students struggle. One seasoned supervisor I interviewed described these students as, "Individuals who show bright talent when led through course work, but when actually deciding a research question, draw a complete blank." Accustomed to seeing the course instructor every week, the student may now think his or her supervisor is unavailable to them. Students at the proposal stage are expected to be self-motivated but have not been given opportunities to practice self-directed learning. They lack confidence to work alone and find it difficult to set and meet self-imposed deadlines.

Developing or Joining a Community of Practice (CoP)

Some students enjoy the solitary work of reading and writing but Golde (2005) identified isolation as a key factor in determining attrition. She made particular note of structural isolation, which involves being isolated in small labs or buildings away from the main faculty. For arts and humanities students, structural isolation means working from home or in remote locations. Students in small departments with few graduate students may experience isolation. Students cannot rely on their programs to mitigate this situation, and as soon as possible, should build a strong peer-support system. Working and meeting regularly with peers can help alleviate the social isolation commonly associated with graduate study. Socializing with others may seem counter-intuitive, but participating in academic writing groups can motivate students to be more productive.

Communities of Practice involve more than friends going out for coffee. CoPs are made up of individuals committed to forming collaborative relationships with others to learn from and teach each other. The community is comprised of individuals who engage in activities and share information and resources. Wenger (1999) provides an example of a community as the French Impressionists who met regularly to discuss the theories and practices of painting, but painted alone in their studios. The practice is the shared repertoire of resources that includes experiences and ways of addressing problems.

Furco and Moely (2012) outline the characteristics of effective CoPs. Participation should be voluntary and meetings should be structured. The members of the group should be goal oriented. Importantly, Furco and Moely point out that the CoP must be a safe place where group members can discuss issues and questions openly and in confidence. Last, the group should be collaborative not competitive.

Working with the Supervisor

Working independently implies that students must write a thesis completely by themselves. Students have supervisors to help guide the research, but it is important to discuss expectations about what guidance they can expect to receive. Moses (1984) identified areas in which students and their supervisors need to set expectations and clarify roles and responsibilities. The proposal stage presents the ideal time for students to initiate a conversation with their supervisors. To begin, students need to determine who is responsible for selecting and approving the research topic. Similarly, they need to determine who will be responsible for other pertinent aspects of the research, such as deciding on a theoretical framework and appropriate methodology. For what aspects of the research project is the supervisor responsible?

What is the supervisors' approach to supervision? Will they read early drafts? Do they want to see the thesis chapter by chapter? Alternatively, is the student expected to work independently to produce several chapters? Some supervisors will only read a complete draft. What level of writing help should the student expect from their supervisor? Will the supervisor read papers the student has written for publication? Is the supervisor responsible for correcting the student's writing? Several supervisors I talked with adamantly refused to act as a copyeditor. One said, "I shouldn't be doing that. My thesis supervisor didn't do that."

Who determines the timeline of research? How often should students and supervisors meet? Who sets appointments and determines the agenda? Who is responsible to keep the students moving toward completion? Not many supervisors clearly articulate these issues so students need to ask and be comfortable with the answers their supervisors provide. If, for example, a supervisor is unwilling to read an early draft and will only read a completed thesis, students need to ask if they can work under these conditions. Some students want and need regular feedback. If the student-supervisor relationship is strained at the proposal stage, it is unlikely to improve with time. It is easier to change supervisors early in the research rather than at later stages.

Finding a Thesis Topic and Formulating a Research Question

Many Master's level students come to graduate school with the goal of learning more about their discipline and are surprised to find the focus is on research (Golde, 2005). Students who are unable to find a topic or question that they are passionate about cannot move forward with a plan of research. One professor I interviewed recalled several meetings with a student who was unable to focus on a topic of research. After one particularly unfruitful meeting, the exasperated student implored him to "Just tell me what to do." Supervisors in some disciplines, such as the natural sciences, may assign the topic and methodology. This can save students valuable time in that they do not have to search for and articulate their own area of research. However, they may not be interested in or excited by the direction of research. Without passion for research, students may not have a sense of ownership of the thesis and feel only relief once it is completed.

Some students may have a vague question, but no real passion for the topic. At the opposite end of the spectrum is the student who is too passionate about an idea and wants to fix a perceived problem. They may set out to prove a point. They do not have a clear sense of what a thesis can do. Or should do. These students believe they already know the answer to their question. While idealism is laudable, this is not the purpose of research. At the heart of research is "search" and to search is to look for something unknown. If the answer is known, it is not necessary to look for it and the data may not support their convictions.

Some master's programs permit students to complete courses in lieu of writing a thesis. Students who have difficulty writing a proposal should take only one or two semesters to complete the task. If they continue to struggle, they should take courses and finish the degree. Despite the number of courses required, it is faster to complete a program by taking courses than to write a thesis when there is no clear direction or a compelling question.

Finding a Research Topic and Methodology

Single (2010) recommends taking into account three constraints when choosing a topic of research: "resources, time, and knowledge" (p. 24). Resources start with the expertise, support, and availability of a supervisor. It is unwise to insist on a topic or research question with which the supervisor is unfamiliar or warns against. Students should find a knowledgeable and sympathetic supervisor or, if one is not to be found, change the topic.

Similarly, the thesis committee should also be supportive of the topic and method. Collectively they have supervised more theses than one student has written, and their advice is intended to ensure success.

Selecting a topic that will sustain one's interest throughout the process requires self-knowledge. Most programs require a letter of intent for admission and it may be helpful to revisit the questions or concerns that brought students to the graduate program in the first place. Self-knowledge considers future goals because the thesis topic and methodology position graduates to compete in the job market. Knowledge includes an understanding of the theoretical and practical concerns of the discipline. Students should identify areas of recurring concern rather than follow trends. Taking on an area or theoretical position that has gone out of favor or is contentious may lower one's chances for future employment. Trends date research and in some cases, render it obsolete.

Writing research questions takes practice and requires many iterations of the same idea. If the answer to the question can be found in an Internet search, it is not a worthy question. Questions suggest methods and ways of analyzing data. The proposal should address what data are needed to answer the question and consider what knowledge is needed to analyze the data. Will the methodology and analysis require specialized knowledge? Are courses available to provide that knowledge?

Institutional support includes the availability of labs, studios, and technical facilities needed to carry out the research. How long will students have access to labs? If others share the lab, how many can be accommodated? There are financial resources to consider. It is important to determine what costs the research will incur and who is responsible to pay them. What costs are students expected to pay and what will the supervisor cover? Research may require travel. Does the university provide funding for off campus research? Are travel funds available for research activities?

Time and resources are closely linked. How long will it take to collect the data? Is there a time limit for student funding? Some universities fund master's students only for their first year and doctoral students for three or four years of study. Supervisors are expected to recruit new students into their programs, and cannot provide funding for students who go beyond a time limit. A realistic time-line for research takes into account supervisor sabbaticals and leaves, and proposes only that which has a reasonable expectation of being delivered. Timelines should take into account time to obtain ethics approval, if necessary, something we discuss in Chapter 7.

Components of the Proposal

A proposal for an action research thesis will differ from one in which a student wishes to test a hypothesis. Most proposals for qualitative research contain an introduction to the proposed inquiry, a review of existing literature to contextualize the inquiry, a methodology section, procedures for research, and a discussion on data analysis. It is important to determine what data will be gathered and how they will be analyzed. Some proposals include a discussion of the study's limitations and the theoretical framework from which the study will be viewed. A quantitative research proposal for testing a hypothesis includes an introduction that defines the research area, the development of a hypothesis, a description of the research design, an explanation of the instruments used for measurement, and a discussion of how the data will be analyzed.

The methodology section should include the methods used to gather data and the study's procedure. Who are the participants? How will they be recruited? What will happen to them as a result of the study? What will they be asked to do? Chapter 7 provides information on core ethical issues. If required, ethics protocol forms should be attached as an appendix. Usually the ethics approval process takes place after the proposal has been accepted, but the form should be consulted while writing the method section.

It is helpful to work out the costs involved in conducting the research. For example, before committing to a study that involves participant interviews, consider the time it will take to transcribe them. If the student plans to pay someone to transcribe, determine the cost of transcribing. Some transcribers charge by the hour and others by the page. In general, an hour interview can generate a 25 page transcript. Focus group interviews usually generate more data and cost more due to their complexity. Admittedly, it is difficult to estimate the length of an interview at the proposal stage. Some focus groups, for example, can be lively while others are terribly quiet.

Generally, students work with their supervisors to develop their proposals. After the supervisor approves a final draft, the proposal may be given to members of the thesis committee. They may meet with the student, or provide feedback to the supervisor. The committee may accept or ask for minor or major revisions. The committee can offer advice that will save time and money, and help the student produce a strong thesis. The student might not agree with the recommendations, but should keep in mind that everyone wants the research to succeed.

CONDUCTING AND WRITING
LITERATURE REVIEWS

INTRODUCTION

To contribute new knowledge to a field of study, students must first establish a comprehensive understanding of existing knowledge. For Holbrook, Bourke, Fairbairn, and Lovat (2007), "The use and application of the literature is at the heart of scholarship—of belonging to the academy" (p. 346). It is the foundation on which the entire thesis rests. However, many students, despite having written many course papers, have no idea of how to write the literature review or even where to start. This chapter explains the goals and purposes of literature reviews and distinguishes types of reviews. It describes how to assess the appropriateness of literature and the steps students take to write the review. It concludes by outlining common mistakes students make when writing literature reviews.

Types of Literature Reviews

This section introduces four ways existing literature is used in research: an annotated bibliography, a literature review, a meta-analysis, and a meta-synthesis. All rely on existing published research, but each serves a different purpose.

An annotated bibliography provides a list of sources for additional reading on the subject. It is usually written as a series of paragraphs, each summarizing a single book or publication, followed by a brief assessment (Jesson, Matheson, & Lacey, 2011). Each summary contains the author's central claims, research questions, and methods used to answer the questions. The sources are arranged alphabetically so they can be easily located for future use. Annotated bibliographies can list potential sources for the literature review.

Literature reviews differ from annotated bibliographies in that the information gleaned from the literature is integrated into paragraphs, and compares and contrasts the findings of the sources. As a chapter, a literature review usually begins with an introductory statement outlining the research question. Ridley (2012) posits that a literature review is both a process and a product. As a process, it involves systematically searching databases for the most current and relevant literature written about the research topic. Kamler and Thomson (2006) note that the word "literature" evokes notions of high culture and instead suggest that it might be more beneficial to think of the process as a review of research. They also question the word "review" which they hold as indicating an onlooker's stance. Instead, they recommend thinking of the process as one that uses or evaluates previously published research.

As a product, the literature review is a written synthesis of what is known about the research topic and provides supporting evidence for the thesis. It is essential for doctoral work that must demonstrate an original contribution to knowledge. For the master's student, the literature review situates the proposed research within the context of other research being conducted in the field. "Finding the gap" is a commonly used metaphor describing the student's task, but this is not easy or obvious. Rather, the literature review indicates what is known and what is yet to be known. Often, students use existing literature to identify problems, justifying the need for their proposed research.

Students must do more than describe the existing literature. Their task is to evaluate the research conducted about their thesis topic and integrate it into their own research. For Randolf (2009), the steps used to conduct and write a literature review mirror the research process. Students start by formulating a question that the literature will answer. They gather data in the form of literature to answer the question, and assess the quality of the evidence found. Finally, they write an analysis and interpretation of the data.

A meta-analysis is both an extensive literature review and a quantitative research method that seeks new knowledge from existing data (Crombie & Davies, 2009). The researcher statistically combines the results from several published papers that report findings from independent quantitative studies addressing the same question. Sometimes referred to as a "systematic review," meta-analyses are frequently used in medicine where several researchers working independently conduct small clinical trials to determine effectiveness of certain treatments.

Meta-analyses require a systematic review of existing literature and researchers must take great care to find all relevant studies on the topic, both published and unpublished. This is sometimes referred to as an "exhaustive search." Additionally, researchers must accurately assess the methodological quality of each study. If an original study is flawed, then the meta-analysis may be flawed as well, a problem referred to as the GIGO principle: "garbage in, garbage out" (Crombie & Davies, 2009, p. 7). A meta-analysis requires that researchers develop a comprehensive search strategy, involving several electronic databases. Crombie and Davies also recommend manually searching a number of key journals to check the references of the papers used for the analysis.

A meta-synthesis is the qualitative equivalent of a meta-analysis in that researchers combine the findings of other qualitative studies to develop new understandings of the research topic and to generalize the findings. This method of research is relatively new, and contested. Generalizing from a single qualitative study is not useful, nor is this the original purpose of a single study. Zimmer (2006) outlines three purposes for a meta-synthesis: theory building, theory explication, and theory development (p. 313). In conducting a meta-synthesis, the researcher brings together a number of studies to produce a more comprehensive understanding of the phenomena being studied (Walsh & Downe, 2005) which allows researchers to generalize their findings (Zimmer, 2006). Not all agree about the merit of this method, arguing that combining several studies destroys the original intent and integrity of each individual study. They argue that the purpose of a qualitative study is to bring a depth of understanding to a single issue, and that the researcher's goal was not to generalize his or her findings (Zimmer, 2006). Others disagree and question the value of producing a single, non-reproducible study. Walsh and Downe (2005) posit the argument for combining findings stating, "…if they continue to produce non-reconcilable islands of knowledge around the same phenomena, they are doomed to irrelevant speculation and to reinventing the wheel" (p. 205).

Students who conduct a meta-analysis and meta-synthesis must guard against publication bias because journals often do not publish studies, as in the case of medical journals, that find no benefit for treatment (Crombie & Davies, 2009). Rothstein, Sutton, and Borenstein (2005) explain that a bias is a term for "what occurs whenever the research that appears in the published literature is systematically unrepresentative of the population of completed studies" and warn that, as a result, those conducting the meta-analysis are "in danger of drawing the wrong conclusion about what the research shows" (p. 1). Qualitative research can also be victim of a publication bias. Petticrew et al. (2008) reviewed the abstracts of qualitative research presented at conferences and found, "Qualitative studies that do not show clear, or striking, or easily described findings may simply disappear from view" (p. 553). In my field, researchers tend to publish success stories, but not failures.

Locating and Evaluating Research

Machi and McEvoy (2012) posit that the literature review is "a written argument that promotes a thesis by building a case from credible evidence based on previous research" (p. 2). Credible is the key word here. Students' task, whether writing for the proposal or the final thesis, is to demonstrate they can separate what is valuable and pertinent from what is not. The fact that a paper has been published does not guarantee its credibility or its usefulness. In most disciplines, credibility is established through the peer-review process, also called "refereed." Peer reviewing consists of the paper being evaluated and approved by two or three reviewers chosen for their expertise in the subject or methodology. Blind peer-review means that neither the reviewers nor author know each other's identity. Peer-review is a discipline's self-regulation process intended to ensure some form of quality control. Most peer-reviewed journals indicate their status on the inside cover, also identifying the editor and listing members of the review board and their university affiliations. Some journals publish instructions to potential authors, specifying their review policies. However, peer-review is an imperfect process. In small fields or niche journals, reviewers can guess the author's identity with a fair amount of accuracy. Reviewers can be biased for or against authors and ideas. Some reviewers are more demanding and scrutinize papers more closely than others. (For a more detailed discussion about the power and politics of the peer-review process, see Chapter 9).

There are increasing numbers of academic journals, all of varying quality. Usually, those regarded as the most prestigious and trusted are called "top-tier" journals. Top-tier journals have the highest impact scores. A journal's impact score is based on the average number of citations per published paper in a particular year or period (Garfield, 2007). It is a ratio between the number of papers published and the number of times other authors cite each paper. Impact scores for over 2550 journals are reported annually in the *Journal Citation Reports* (JCR), which is prepared and published by Thomson Reuters, a multinational mass media and information firm. Librarians use impact scores to help them determine which journals to purchase and authors use them to decide where to send papers for publication (Garfield, 2007).

Top-tier journals publish papers by well-known scholars. In some programs, having a paper accepted for publication is a requirement for receiving tenure, promotion, or research grants. These journals give tenure committees and granting agencies a standard from which to judge faculty research. Subsequently, top-tier journals receive many submissions and are very competitive. They also have high rejection rates. There is controversy around impact as some authors have discovered how to inflate their scores by citing their own research. Additionally, there have been reported instances of "coercing citation." This entails requests by editors, or reviewers, to add citations to a submitted manuscript or risk rejection by that journal. Wilhite and Fong (2012) analyzed 6672 responses from a survey sent to researchers in economics, sociology, psychology, and business (marketing, finance, management, and accounting) and found a majority of respondents said they have "add[ed] superfluous citations before submitting to a journal known to coerce" (p. 542). The practice of using impact numbers is an imperfect measure of quality and as Eugene Garfield (2007), inventor of the system, writes, "Obviously, a better evaluation would involve actually reading each article for quality..." (p. 69). In sum, students should begin their literature searches with peer-reviewed articles from high impact journals, but they should read critically and determine the quality of each article for themselves.

The number of research journals has risen exponentially due in part to the increasing demands for graduate students to publish to obtain academic positions and post-doctoral funding (Billig, 2013). Many of these journals have low-impact scores and are considered to be second or third tier. They may publish edited papers as opposed to peer-reviewed. In these cases, the journal's editor decides which papers will be published and what, if any, changes are required. However the papers published in these journals should not be dismissed, and students should judge each on its own merit. For example, student researchers do not have the time or money to run large clinical trials, but may nonetheless, have some important preliminary findings.

But Is It Research?

Just as all research is not peer-reviewed, not everything published is based on research. Some journals publish opinion papers, which may or may not be peer-reviewed. Additionally, they may publish keynote speeches without editing. These individuals may be award recipients and hold status in the field, and are selected by their association's executive board members to provide a keynote address for a conference. The resulting paper may be invited and may be based on opinion gained from long time participation in the field. Metcalfe (2003) notes, "if the authors are giving their opinion about some social situation based, not on specific empirical research, but rather 'long experience' then the value of this 'long experience' needs to be justified" (para. 31). Metcalfe gives validity to long-time experience but asks, "Do the authors compare their opinion with others, do they openly address counter opinions, and are they free from bias, prejudice, inconsistency and publication opportunism?" (para. 32).

Commissioned reports, governmental policies, working papers, and conference proceedings are referred to as "grey literature" (Jesson, Matheson, & Lacey, 2011; Ridley, 2012). Conference proceedings are peer-reviewed for inclusion in the conference, but this may be based on as little as a 230–300 word abstract. Petticrew et al. (2008) conducted a systematic review of databases and found that less than half of the research presented at conferences was subsequently published. Ten researchers whose papers were not published were then interviewed to find what happened to the papers. Those interviewed gave a variety of reasons such as lost interest, and didn't have the time to write the paper. One reported he or she "'lost heart' after poor reviews" (p. 553). If students elect to include a conference paper in the literature review, caution should be taken to ascertain if the paper was published at a later date.

Government policies and reports may not indicate the sources the authors used to produce the written document and may have political biases. Generally, books are not peer-reviewed. Anthologies, which are compilation of chapters written by several authors on a given topic, are usually written at the invitation of the book's editor. The editor may be a well-known expert or a newcomer to the field. The quality of each chapter may vary and there are no impact factors to guide the student. In these cases, students must read carefully to consider the quality and credibility of each chapter.

Internet blogs should be omitted from the literature review. This is not to say the information provided by these venues is inaccurate. The Internet is a democratic place that allows people to voice their opinions without being silenced by the gatekeepers of the peer-review process. Anyone can put anything online. However, many top-tier peer-reviewed journals also are published as online sources, so publishing online does not automatically discount the quality and credibility of research found there.

The literature review should consist mainly of primary sources, which are original studies, informed by direct observation or other research methods that contain original data. Secondary sources are interpretations of primary sources. In this sense, literature reviews are secondary sources. Tertiary literature is the further distilling of material to form textbooks and guidebooks. These resources may be informative, but students should take care in evaluating them before including them in a literature review.

Students must be critical of what they read and include in their literature review. However, being critical does not mean being overly negative or disrespectful. Kamler and Thomson (2006) advise, "But to be critical is also respectful of what others have done, to look at what they contributed, rather than going on the attack" (p. 40). They suggest asking what the research contributes, rather than point out how it fails. In my view, a good critique identifies both the strengths and weaknesses of published research. Students need to demonstrate they can judge the quality of a publication rather than report the findings as fact. It is important to examine claims made by the author and evaluate the evidence used to support those claims. What methodology was used? What are the data and how were they collected? Do the data support the claims? Does the author make generalizations based on a small descriptive study? What are the study's limitations? Is bias evident? It is important to distinguish between an assertion and that which provides evidence to support the claim. Baumeister and Leary (1997) recommend, "Group or section critiques are often useful because many studies on the same topic may be subject to similar flaws or criticisms" (p. 318).

Where to Start and When to Stop

A literature review should start with an appointment with a research librarian. This is key because he or she can provide expertise on how to source and judge the quality of the literature. Librarians will identify specialized databases and provide instruction on how to use referencing systems, such as EndNote or RefWorks, to help manage the resources. These systems automatically format the papers, though caution should be taken to ensure the citations accurately conform to the guidelines of a particular style, such as APA, Chicago, or AMA.

Fink (2010) provides four key words, which help focus a search: systematic, explicit, comprehensive, and reproducible (p. 15). Students must systematically search relevant databases and explicitly communicate their decisions to the reader. It is important to keep detailed records of searches, both to establish an audit trail and to avoid duplicating searches. Make a note of each database searched, when it was searched, what years of publication were covered, and which publications were included. Keep track of key words used in each search. This careful note taking will save time and having to repeat the search years later when students have forgotten they already did it.

Students should make notes as they read, and keep them organized. Special care should be taken to distinguish between a direct quote and a paraphrased idea. Plagiarism can happen when students inadvertently copy a direct quote into their paper, thinking it to be something they wrote. Ensure that all direct quotes have quotation marks followed by the page from which the quote was taken. Create a list of every article and book read, with notes and citations for each, no matter how pointless it might seem. This is especially important at the beginning of the search. There's nothing more annoying than getting half way through an article and realizing you'd already read it three years ago, or remembering a paper but not being able to find it.

I take Fink's notion of explicit to mean that the student should determine the parameters of their literature search. Students are not expected to review all the literature ever written on a subject. It should be clear that exhaustion describes the review, not the student. Reviewing papers from a specific period of time, or using a specific methodology may provide useful limits. A narrowly focused review can provide more depth than one that is far-reaching. Students must explicitly identify and defend their criteria for inclusion and exclusion of the resources they find (Randolf, 2009). Fink (2010) identifies a comprehensive review as one that supplements electronic searches with reviews of references in the identified literature and manual searches of references and journals. The reference list at the end of a paper can often point to something that might not be found otherwise. Last, a review is reproducible when the reader follows the student's path to search literature and arrives with similar results.

Theoretically, the review stops when the reviewer reaches saturation, which means he or she finds no additional papers that provide new information. For the student, this may seems like the literature review can go on forever, and they would be correct. New information is added daily. So when can the search stop? Randolf (2009) points out that a literature review is a labor intensive process, and estimates that doctoral students will need between three to six months to complete the task. Booth, Papaioannou, and Sutton (2012) recommend students spend between nine months to a year to do so. I recommend master's students devote a semester to writing the literature review. This is based on the practical notion that, in a two-year program, a quarter of the student's time should be devoted to locating existing literature for their proposal. Clearly, a meta-analysis or meta-synthesis, which is also the methodology for the research, should take a greater amount of time to complete. However, reviewing the literature is an on-going process that stops when the final thesis is submitted. Literature is constantly updated and added to the thesis when it is relevant.

Writing the Review

When writing the review, students should begin by telling the readers, in this case the supervisor and thesis committee, what the literature review is about. What questions did the existing literature answer? Next, provide the details of the way the literature was searched. Describe the parameters for the search. What was included and what was intentionally omitted? For example, were commissioned reports included? Why or why not? This audit trail includes the databases and key words used for the search. The audit trail gives the readers confidence that the search was systematic and comprehensive. If little was found on the topic, the supervisor may be able to suggest alternative key terms or additional databases that will yield more results.

Randolf (2009) lists three common ways to organize the review: the historical format, the conceptual format, and methodological format. The historical review is used to demonstrate changes in understanding, and resources are presented chronologically. This is used when students wish to show progress or demonstrate how ideas change or theories develop over time. The conceptual approach, or a theoretically focused review, is structured around various theories posited in the literature. A methodological review presents the paper like empirical research, in that it provides an introduction, the method, and results and discussion. When assessing the literature, critique groups of studies rather than each one individually. When using any of these organizational structures, address how other researchers' work informs the proposed research. How will your research build on, or fill the gap? What problems suggested by the literature will your research address?

Common Mistakes Made in Literature Reviews

Holbrook et al. (2007) examined 1310 written reports from external theses examiners for 501 doctoral candidates across five Australian universities. They found three problems most commonly identified with the literature review of completed theses: inadequate or missing key literature, inaccuracy, and poor use.

An inadequate literature review is one that is missing key literature, relies too heavily on secondary sources, or includes poor examples. It is not uncommon to attend a conference and hear a novice researcher make the claim that little research has been conducted on his or her topic. Inevitably, someone is sitting in the back of the room, arms crossed, waiting for the presentation to end to point to the fact that she or he had written the definitive book on the subject. In some cases, the researcher did not conduct a thorough literature review or had narrowed the search to keywords that did not encompass the topic. However, even the most careful researcher may miss something, so these suggestions should be regarded as constructive criticism.

A literature review should use primary sources and should never contain secondary citations. For example, a student may cite John Dewey (1930) but take the citation from Smith, who quoted Dewey in her text. In order to cite Dewey, students must read Dewey, no matter how painful that may be. They may not recount Proust's lovely story about sweet scented *madeleines* unless they have read both volumes of *À la recherche du temps perdu*. Metcalfe (2003), using the metaphor of a courtroom trial, considers secondary citation as "hearsay evidence" (p. 9). He makes the general rule: "Do not reference an article unless you have read it yourself" (p. 10). It is essential that students are able to demonstrate an in-depth knowledge of all the literature they cite and committee members may question such knowledge during an oral defense.

Inaccurate references include omitting or inconsistently citing a reference. This includes misspelling an author's name, listing the wrong publication date, or misquoting the author. Take care that every citation used in the text also appears in the references and vice versa. Thesis examiners see sloppy citations as red flags alerting them to the possibility of plagiarism (Holbrook et al., 2007). Citing the exact page number and ensuring all information is correct is essential. Correcting citations after the thesis has been written is time consuming. It is more efficient to do it right the first time.

The following chapter discusses plagiarism and ways to avoid it when working with source materials, but there are other negative ways in which students may use the literature on which their thesis is based. Poor use can mean that key literature was intentionally omitted because it disagreed with the student's premise. This includes "cherry picking" quotes that agree with the premise, but are taken out of their original context.

Poor use also includes confusing an assertion with evidence. An author may make a strong statement, but students must ask how the author came to the conclusion? What data was provided to support the claim? Simply repeating the author's claim does not make it true. Baumeister and Leary (1997) point out a common mistake is citing a study's conclusion without discussing the methodology or supporting evidence. There is a difference between reporting on what a paper or researcher said and providing an analysis of the research. Reporting takes for granted the writer did proper research, whereas analysis examines the research methods and findings.

Stringing and Dumping

Authors, responding to the word limitations for published papers, have developed short-cut strategies to write as much as possible in the least amount of space. Two of those strategies are stringing and dumping. Described by Metcalfe (2003), dumping involves writing a statement, followed by numerous sources. It is used when a topic has been taken up by a number of researchers. The following example is taken from Hayes and Introna's (2005) paper on plagiarism.

> The issue of academic integrity within higher education has received considerable attention in the literature over recent years. (Carroll & Appleton, 2001; Decert, 1993; Harris, 2001; Howard, 1993, 1995; Kolich, 1983; Lanthrop, 2000; Martin, 1994;...) (p. 213)

By dumping the names and dates of the sources, the authors demonstrate that they have done due diligence by finding articles written on their topic, and support their assertion that "The issue of academic integrity within higher education has received considerable attention over recent years" (p. 213). However, they do not discuss what kind of attention was given or explain what each found. Collectively, what did these authors contribute to our understanding of the topic? Perhaps they assume readers are familiar with the literature or, if interested, will follow-up on the sources cited.

An example of stringing comes from Park (2003):

> The plagiarist has been describes as a "thought thief" (Whiteneck, 2002) or "intellectual shoplifter" (Stebelman, 1998), charged with having committed "forgery" (Groom, 2000), "theft of ideas" (Hopkins, 1993) and a "crime." (Franke, 1993, p. 473)

Stringing and dumping are forms of name-dropping. Neither develops the ideas covered in the material cited nor indicates if the citations are from evidence or opinion. The practice has become the culture for a number of academic journals, but the practice does nothing to advance scholarship or knowledge.

Students may dump and string because they are imitating the common culture of journal writing. They may be afraid they will be called out for missing a key piece of literature so they are over zealous to include anything ever written about the subject. But, simply citing something does not demonstrate an understanding of what was written nor provide a critique of it. It only demonstrates the ability to find articles. Students are responsible for everything they include in their thesis and must defend why they include each citation. Is the research significant to the student's research and is it reliable research? If poor research is cited, then students should indicate the problems or limitations of the research. If the thesis is built on a weak foundation, it will not stand.

This chapter closes by reminding students that the process of searching for literature does not end with the proposal. Students need to update their literature to include any new and relevant research published during the research period. This is particularly important for those in fields, such as humanities and education, where the thesis process can take many years. The literature review should not look like a time capsule of the year the proposal was written. Students may need to conduct additional searches if their data suggest findings that differ from the original focus. Sources need to be constantly added to, and in some cases, deleted as the research narrows. After the initial literature review is written, students should devote a specific amount of time to refreshing their search. Doing so will also help to keep a keen interest in the sometimes long task of writing a thesis.

MAINTAINING ACADEMIC INTEGRITY

INTRODUCTION

Universities are knowledge producers. Cheating, in its various manifestations, damages the integrity of the knowledge produced and destroys the reputation of students, professors, and the university. Academic integrity is concerned with moral and ethical issues, including respecting other's dignity, rights, and property. Violations can include cheating on exams, falsifying documents, and unauthorized collaboration. This chapter deals specifically with plagiarism as it applies to thesis writing. Most universities focus their efforts on educating about and preventing plagiarism at the undergraduate level, as the majority of academic misconduct cases involve undergraduate students. Professors assume graduate students have learned how to properly cite as undergraduates. Their syllabi warn of the consequences of plagiarism, but rarely do they discuss what the misconduct entails. This chapter draws on academic literature concerning plagiarism and my experience as a code administrator[1] to help students avoid committing academic misconduct when writing a thesis. Last, I offer advice on how to deal with a plagiarism charge.

At the most basic level, plagiarism is defined as claiming knowledge that is not one's own. It can be lifted be from another student's work or from a published source. It can also refer to images, formulae, music, and other forms (Sutherland-Smith, 2005). "Self-plagiarism," occurs when students submit the same paper or work for two courses without their instructors' permission. This is also called "multiple submission."

Plagiarism can be deliberate or unintentional, but most university codes of conduct treat all offences as deliberate. It is difficult, if not impossible, to distinguish between the deceptive and the desperate. Most code administrators report that they cannot ascertain whether students intended to cheat or if they are guilty of sloppy paraphrasing or have poor referencing skills (Pecorari, 2003; Sutherland-Smith, 2005). Students are responsible for knowing and abiding by citation rules, and pleading ignorance will not make an offence disappear.

Intentional plagiarism is akin to premeditated murder, in that it is deliberate and planned (Park, 2003). At its worst, it involves buying a paper from an

Internet source or from another student, or hiring a ghostwriter to write a customized paper. Some ghostwriters use dated print sources to avoid being caught by online detection software. Professors know students use online sources and are suspect of a paper with many older references. Plagiarism can also involve copying a passage verbatim from another source without crediting the author. Unintentional plagiarism, on the other hand, might mean a student forgot to cite a paraphrased section of a paper or inadvertently left the page number off a direct quotation. Intentional or not, a plagiarism charge carries the weight of a moral failing.

International students have a high risk of being charged with plagiarism, and the literature suggests they make up the up the greatest number of misconduct cases (Abasi & Graves, 2008; Gu & Brooks, 2008; Park, 2003). Researchers offer conflicting perspectives on why this is the case. Hayes and Introna (2005), for example, suggest that Asian students hold different views of what academic writing entails and have high respect for authority. Accordingly, these students state the author's words and are reluctant to paraphrase or critique them. Gu and Brooks (2008) refute this claim, suggesting this is an overgeneralization and, in some cases, not based on fact.

I believe international students get caught plagiarizing because it is easy to detect copying in their written work. Course instructors are alerted to the possibility of plagiarism when the submitted work displays an inconsistent writing style. The copied section differs in style and tone from the rest of the paper. Students, who normally write short, simple statements, arouse suspicion when they suddenly use compound sentences with the correct use of colons and semicolons. Professors take note when the vocabulary and fluency of the written work is in sharp contrast with the student's oral skills. At times, plagiarism is a result of poor time management. Students who study in languages different from their own must spend more time reading and writing than do their native speaking counterparts. However, graduate programs are competitive and international students are not given additional time to complete assignments. I also suspect that professors report international students more than others because they do not experience a bond with them. Often, these students are shy to participate in class because they have little confidence in their speaking skills, and they do not share a common popular culture with their professors. These students cannot discuss the professor's favorite film during informal gatherings. Professors are less likely to take formal action against students with which they have a personal connection. The problem is acerbated in that some students are reluctant to defend themselves against the charges, even when they are innocent. They may not know how to defend themselves, thinking that if they make excuses, it will make things worse.

Graduate students in sciences and technology programs are also at a risk of plagiarizing. Unlike those in the humanities and social sciences, science and technology students cannot use direct quotations for technical writing (Eckel, 2010). For them, paraphrasing requires mastery of the original concept and the ability to synthesis it in one's own words. Some students who have not mastered these skills use a writing strategy known as patchwriting (Howard, 1993). Like a patchwork quilt, a patchwritten text is made with existing bits and pieces taken from other sources stitched together to make a cohesive statement. Students may cut and paste a phrase, then use a thesaurus to find substitutes for key words. Howard et al. (2010) hold that these students do not intend to deceive, but rather their writing is indicative of a poor understanding of the language or the concepts it describes. These students mimic academic language but cannot synthesize the writing and ideas of others. They suggest that patchwriting is a strategy that students use until they find their own voice.

How Can Plagiarism Be Prevented?

The best way to avoid plagiarism is to be proactive. Nearly all universities have explicit, written policies on plagiarism and students are advised to become familiar with them before writing their first assignment. Many times, students are not aware of plagiarism rules, particularly when citing their own work. Not all undergraduate programs teach proper citation and some are quite lax in what they deem acceptable. Libraries often give workshops on citation practices at the beginning of each academic year. Although these workshops are geared toward undergraduates, they can serve as a refresher course for graduate students. Students should not take for granted that they know how to cite properly. When writing from sources, analyze rather than describe. After each point, ask, "How do I know this?" "Is this from personal experience, my own research, or did I read about it?"

Students may address the same topic in two or more courses. Students may wish to combine the courses to work on a large project rather than two that are smaller and unrelated. In this case, transparency is necessary to avoid multiple submission or self-plagiarism. Before turning in the same or similar work to two professors, discuss plans to do so with both. Offer to submit both papers to each professor, which allows them to see how much work was repeated or overlapped.

Be cautious when working with several digital documents, and avoid cutting and pasting among them (Hayes & Introna, 2005). In fact, never cut and paste into a document thinking you will paraphrase later. Some students attempt to keep track of these sections by using large font or highlighting them in color, but invariably forget them when they "select all" and change the font. Quoted passages are subsumed into the text and students forget to put quotation marks around the passage and cite it. Keep copies of drafts and be able to show the work. In art and design, be prepared to show sketches to demonstrate how found images were transformed.

What Happens If You Are Charged with Plagiarism?

Being charged with plagiarism is every student's nightmare and the word alone can cause extreme anxiety. Typically, course instructors initiate the process when they submit evidence of misconduct, usually consisting of the student's paper and a copy of the original source to the department chair or code administrator. If a formal charge is made, students are often notified by registered mail. The code administrator investigates the charge, and frequently calls the student in for an interview. The code administrator either upholds or dismisses the charge. If the charge is dismissed, all records are destroyed. The consequences of a guilty verdict can range in severity from a letter of reprimand to expulsion. Students tend to fear the worst, but most first infractions do not result in expulsion. Students may be given a failing grade on the assignment or on the course, and a letter of reprimand. The letter serves as a warning to the students and as a record. Should they commit a second offense, the consequence is more severe.

Student advocacy groups can support students through this stressful process. Although some students are too ashamed to let others know about the charge, those working in these programs are trained to help students prepare their defense. In some cases, a student advocate will accompany them to the interview. They can also tell students what not to do. Some actions, such as demanding to meet with the professor immediately, can make things worse. If you are guilty, admit it. The code administrator may suggest ways to prevent another charge.

Plagiarism is often treated as a singular issue when it is, in fact, quite complex. Unintentional plagiarism is a symptom of a problem, but many treat it with retribution rather than rehabilitation. In most cases, the problems are poor writing and time management skills. While I agree that only the student can know the intention, people do make mistakes. A plagiarism charge does not have to signal the end of one's academic career. Students can learn from their mistakes and go on to be successful graduates, contributing to their field of study.

NOTE

[1] The primary role of a code administrator is to investigate charges against students brought by professors. In this way, professors police their courses and code administrators act as judges who determine the consequences.

CHOOSING A METHODOLOGY

INTRODUCTION

To carry out research, students choose the methodology that best answers their question. On the surface, it seems easy. However, books about methodology take up entire floors of libraries and there is a dizzying array of approaches and conflicting ways to describe them. Tradition, inquiry, genre, strategy, methodology, and method are just some of the terms authors use to describe the same activity. Finding a way out of the methodology labyrinth can be daunting for the graduate student who just needs to "get it right."

Students need to do more than choose a method and collect data. They need to understand the underlying beliefs of the their chosen research tradition. All methodologies have strengths and limitations and each brings with it ethical values and principles on how to conduct research. Methodologies embody the values and assertions from centuries of philosophical debate. Understandably, unpacking the antecedents takes time and most students want to do research, not read about it. However, if students are aware of the tensions within a methodology, and of its critics, they can make a more informed decision about using it.

Using Russian nesting dolls as a metaphor, this chapter unpacks the concepts of epistemology, methodology, and method. Next, it offers a brief explanation of the various approaches that students might take for their research. It looks at the concepts ascribed to each methodology, describes its basic values and guiding principles, and considers the criteria each has established for judgment. It returns to Single's (2010) three constraints: "resources, time, and knowledge" to consider the practical aspects of carrying out research (p. 24). It concludes with strategies to write a methodology section or chapter.

Each field or discipline has preferred research methodologies and methods. Art historians and mechanical engineers approach research in very different ways. Moreover, individual members of each discipline frequently disagree on best practices. Fierce battles, with name-calling and dismissing a colleague's methodology as unscholarly, are waged at departmental meetings, cocktail parties, and on the printed pages of journals. Many innocent students have been caught in the crossfire of these methodological battles, and those who unknowingly put members of warring factions on thesis committees find themselves in the position of having to choose sides or negotiate a truce.

Epistemology

The choice of a methodology starts by asking, "What do I want to know?" By asking this question, students enter into the initial phase of research that deals with how different traditions regard knowledge. Epistemology is the theory of how we know the world and of how we gain knowledge of it (Denzin & Lincoln, 2011). It also takes into account the role of the researcher as one who gathers and constructs knowledge. Epistemology asks, "Who can be a knower?" (Leavy, 2015, p. 3). Do we know something because we observed it? Do we know something because we deduced it through logic? There are many ways of knowing, and each is an integral part of a methodology. Is knowledge something that exists and can be discovered or do we construct knowledge? The doctoral student, who is tasked with producing new knowledge, must consider the question, "What is knowledge and how do I go about acquiring it"?

There are many ideas about what constitutes knowledge and how we acquire it, but most graduate research deals with either empiricism or constructivism. Empiricism is based on knowing through the senses. We know something if we see it or experience it. Research is intended to produce evidence of what we can observe and measure. Some empiricists adhere to positivism, and according to Johnson and Christensen (2013), "They assume that there is a reality to be observed and that rational observers who look at the same phenomenon will basically agree on its existence and characteristics" (p. 36). Positivists hold that an objective truth exists, and is knowable if researchers use a logical, systematic scientific methodology to find it. The researcher exists apart from the research and attempts to be objective and free from biases. Post-positivism emerged from positivism. Although universal truths are thought to exist, post-positivists believe researchers can never represent that truth with complete accuracy (Spencer, Pryce, & Walsh, 2015). The researchers' and participants' biases and the research design affect the outcome of inquiry.

Constructivism, on the other hand, holds that knowledge is acquired through social interaction (Denzin & Lincoln, 2011). The constructivist's point of view is both pragmatic and relativistic. For the pragmatic, something is true when it works. The relativists hold that people construct reality in different ways and the goal of research is to understand, but not predict. The researcher is an integral part of the research and influences the research at all stages from collecting evidence to interpreting it.

There are, admittedly, many approaches to research besides post-positivism and constructivism. Creswell (2013) adds transformative and critical frameworks, among others. A transformative framework holds that knowledge reflects power relationships in society and the purpose of knowledge creation is to improve the lives of those marginalized by that society. Critical frameworks include examples such as feminist, critical race theory, queer theory, and disability theory. For each framework, "Reality is known through the study of social structures, freedom and oppression, power, and control" (Creswell, 2013, p. 37).

The Methodology

The next question students must consider is, "What methodology is best suited to produce the knowledge to answer my research question?" What constitutes a methodology is not a universally accepted idea. Students are correct when they ask, for example, if a case study is an approach, a strategy, a methodology, or a method. The answer is "Yes." Creswell (2013) uses the term "approaches" to describe that which Wheeldon and Ahlberg (2012) call methodologies. For Wheeldon and Ahlberg, a methodology is "the design, strategy, or plan of action required to gather and analyze data" (p. 5). It is the sum total of the theory and assumptions of research, and the procedures for which it carries it out. Methodologies suggest the ways for acquiring—and criteria for judging—knowledge. Each carries epistemological assumptions about how we think we know something and how we go about searching for knowledge.

Carter and Little (2007) posit that epistemology has three main influences on methodology. First, it influences the relationship between the researcher and the participants. Are participants the subject of the research or are they active co-creators of knowledge? Second, epistemology affects the way researchers collect and analyze data. Does the researcher use a predesigned, repeatable method, or does the researcher collect data through reflective iterations? Third, Carter and Little point out that, "epistemology influences form, voice, and representation in the method" (p. 1322). Is the final research written in first person or third person? Will the data be presented as words or images?

Method

Methodology and method are often used interchangeably, but they are not the same thing. A method is how the methodology is carried out

(Carter & Little, 2007, p. 1318). Methods are the techniques and strategies that allow researchers to collect evidence. For example, in order to enact ethnography, the researcher uses participant observation and interviewing methods. The method answers the question, "What tools do I use to collect evidence for my research?" "How do I put methodology in action?" Each methodology has preferred methods. Students overcome an important hurdle in their graduate studies when they can see the relationship between their research question, their methodology, and the theories of knowledge.

The following section briefly describes the quantitative and qualitative approaches, and discusses action and arts research methodologies in greater detail.

QUANTITATIVE RESEARCH

Quantitative research lets researchers know and measure the relationship between an independent variable and a dependent or outcome variable (Hopkins, 2000). This relationship provides the basis for predictions, and "can be used to describe or note numerical changes in measurable characteristics of a population of interest" (Kraska, 2010, p. 1167). Typically, quantitative research results are described numerically. Quantitative research is used in many disciplines, including medicine, psychology, and education. Quantitative research follows the confirmatory scientific method in which a researcher states the hypotheses, tests it with empirical data, and accepts or rejects the hypothesis (Johnson & Christensen, 2013; Kraska, 2010). Quantitative researchers gather empirical evidence but never find conclusive proof for their hypothesis. This may disappoint the policy makers, as well as students who begin their thesis journey with the goal of proving a point. Quantitative research establishes the relationship between variables. A variable is a condition that can take different values (Johnson & Christensen, 2013). Quantitative research can be experimental, quasi experimental, or non-experimental. Non-experimental research methods include causal comparative, correlation studies, and survey research.

Experimental Research

There are many types of variables but the most well known are independent and dependent. Experimental research allows researchers to manipulate the independent variable and measure its relationship to the dependent variable. A cause and effect relationship is established when the independent is responsible for the change in the dependent variable (Johnson & Christensen, 2013). For example, researchers might ask if museum visits can improve students' critical thinking skills (Bowen, Greene, & Kisida, 2013). In this case, the independent variable is the trip to the museum, and the dependent variable is critical thinking skills.

Experimentation allows researchers to predict and generalize their findings to similar situations. When a celebrity doctor endorses the latest miracle weight loss drug, we trust that it has been rigorously tested on others; if it worked for them, it will work for us. Researchers randomly assign participants to groups that allow for comparison. Typically, one group receives the treatment and the other receives a placebo. In clinical drug trials, a placebo looks the same as the drug being tested. Researchers are "blind" when they do not know which participants in the study received the treatment and which were assigned to a control group. Double blind means neither the researcher nor participants know to which group they were assigned.

Experimental research has an allure because many people look for cause/effect relationships. Teachers may ask, "If I adopt the latest teaching tool, will my students learn more? Does providing rubrics at the beginning of an assignment affect creativity?" Although experimental research is attractive to many researchers, it is difficult, if not impossible, to carry out in real world settings such as schools and hospitals. Researchers must control all variables and keep all factors constant so they can study one variable at a time. Extraneous variables are those not controlled for in an experiment, and they can influence the outcome. Teacher and student enthusiasm or resistance can affect how well a treatment works. Participants may want to please the researcher, or sabotage the study. Extraneous variables are said to be confounding when they provide an alternative explanation for any changes discovered (Kovera, 2010).

Quasi-Experimental Research

In addition to difficulty in controlling variables, researchers in many disciplines cannot randomly assign participants to groups. In schools, for example, groups are preexisting. Moreover, researchers cannot withhold a treatment from participants if they believe it works. It is unethical to not give children effective instruction or withhold life saving drugs from patients. In these cases, researchers resort to quasi-experimental methods and matching groups may be used (Kraska, 2010). For example, Bowen, Greene, and Kisida (2013) conducted a "large-scale, random-assignment study of school tours to the museum" (p. 38). As researchers, they could not randomly select children. Rather, they randomly selected intact groups of children. Of the 3811 children in the study, some groups of children went to museums, and others did not. The researchers examined data from the treatment group and its paired control group, and "were able to determine that strong causal relationships do in fact exist between arts education and a range of desirable outcomes"(p. 43). To achieve this, they used similar scores on pretests to ensure the groups were matched adequately (Kraska, 2010). After the museum visits, they administered the same posttest to each group, noting differences in scores. Kraska (2010) notes that nonrandomized control group, pretest, and posttest design is weaker than a true experiment, but is more convenient for the researcher and more palatable to stakeholders.

Nonexperimental Research

Whereas an experimental study establishes causality, a nonexperimental study establishes an association between the variables (Hopkins, 2000). Referred to as descriptive research, this kind of research examines what is observable. The researcher makes no intervention, but instead studies something as it exists. This research answers "What is...?" type questions.

Comparison studies When an experiment is not feasible or desirable, researchers can use causal comparative methods. Johnson and Christensen (2013) call this a "weaker method" (p. 43) and note that the word "causal" is misleading because with these methods researchers can only show a relationship. Causal comparative studies are "ex post facto" meaning after the fact (Brewer & Kuhn, 2010). Typically, researchers compare two groups, one that experienced a variable and a control group that did not. Researchers are unable to control for extraneous variables.

Correlation studies are used to explore two variables but researchers cannot say one causes the other, nor can they distinguish between the independent variable and the dependent variable (Kraska, 2010). A positive correlation is said to exist when two variables move in the same direction. Vigen's (2015) amusing book, *Spurious Correlations* demonstrates that one cannot attribute cause and effect by simply showing the relationship's existence. For example, the per capita consumption of mozzarella cheese and civil engineering doctorates awarded are both on the rise (r=09586). However, correlation research can provide data for future experimental research concerning two variables. While correlation and causal comparison studies cannot demonstrate cause, they can show that two variables are unrelated or have a weak relationship, which informs future hypotheses.

Survey research is used to collect descriptive data drawn from a sample population to generalize to a larger population (Hopkins, 2000). It is the most ubiquitous form of inquiry. We are asked our opinion on a variety of matters, such as our perception of service at a restaurant or how we plan to vote in the upcoming election. At the end of each semester, students are surveyed on their perceptions of instructor effectiveness. Some graduate students may be drawn to survey research because it appears to be an easy and low cost way to gather data. They could not be more wrong. Survey research is complex and expensive in time and money.

A questionnaire is the main instrument of survey research (Trobia, 2008). Questionnaires are often confused with interviews, but the two are not synonymous. Questionnaires are a set of carefully worded standardized questions called items. They include a cover letter informing potential respondents about the research, and instructions if the questionnaire is self-administered. The goal of survey research is to gather data from many people in order to determine averages. Questionnaires must be carefully written because the researcher cannot follow up for clarity or more information. The items need to be clear to the people responding to them. In addition, the questions should not lead the respondent in any way and all responses should be "exhaustive and mutually exclusive" (Trobia, p. 635). Questions can be either open-ended or closed-ended. Open-ended questions allow respondents to express their thoughts in words, while closed-ended items are presented as a statement to which the respondent agrees or disagrees by selecting answers from a rating scale. For example, a Likert-type scale, used ubiquitously, offers five choices ranging from strongly agree to strongly disagree.

Before sending out a questionnaire, researchers need to make several pilot tests and then follow up with respondents to ensure clarity and ease of use. To be valid or meaningful, a questionnaire should measure what the researchers intended to measure. Researchers can start by establishing face validity, which asks experts, "On the face of things, do the investigators reach the correct conclusion?" (Garber, 2008, p. 471). Establishing the validity of a questionnaire can take several iterations. Students can save time and ensure a higher validity by using a pre-existing questionnaire that has been validated by its use in a number of studies.

Beam (2012) criticizes survey research as not providing reliable data because of low responder rates and the inaccuracy of the responses. The vast majority of people who are sent the questionnaire do not complete it. Those that do can give inaccurate responses, either unintentionally or intentionally. For instance, people underestimate the number of calories they consume and overestimate their amount of daily exercise.

Criteria for Judgment for Quantitative Research

Validity is the assurance that the study measures what it claims to study and the conclusions are supported by the data collected by the researcher (Rolfe, 2006). When Bowen et al. (2013) made the claim for improved critical thinking skills in the study mentioned above, they used an existing and validated critical-thinking check-list. Reliability is validity's twin concept. Reliability means that there is a likelihood the same results would be found in another study using the same methodology, in this case the existing and validated critical thinking checklist. Reliability indicates consistency and replicability (Rolfe, 2006). Together, validity and reliability allow researchers to generalize the finding of their studies to other situations. When Bowen et al. (2013) claim that "an arts experience can have a significant impact on critical thinking skills" (p. 43), they generalized this claim beyond Arkansas, where the study was conducted.

Objectivity is important in quantitative research and researchers take care to avoid bias. It is disturbing to the public to hear news that a company paid a researcher to test their product. A researcher might use a standardized questionnaire, as opposed to a one-on-one interview to collect data to avoid researcher bias.

Students considering quantitative research for thesis research need training in technical and scientific writing and a strong grounding in statistics. Unlike qualitative research, quantitative research should never be described as "messy." However, in certain fields of study and for certain questions students have in any field, only quantitative research is appropriate.

QUALITATIVE RESEARCH

Qualitative methodologies bring deeper understanding to human behavior and to people's lived experiences (Denzin & Lincoln, 2011). Qualitative research, which encompasses a number of methodologies, is not the opposite of quantitative research, nor should one be characterized as being about numbers and the other about words or images. They are epistemologically different. Qualitative research is usually associated with the constructivism, or the socially constructed nature of knowledge. Individuals or groups construct meaning over time and experience and the researcher's goal is to "make sense or interpret phenomena in terms of the meaning people bring to them" (Denzin & Lincoln, p. 3). Qualitative researchers may also employ transformative or critical frameworks, such as feminism, Queer theory, and critical race theory, among others. Typically, qualitative studies involve a smaller number of participants than does quantitative research and is carried out in natural settings.

Qualitative researchers take a holistic approach to inquiry, characterized by extensive researcher involvement in the collection and interpretation of data. The researcher is considered to be the research instrument in that she or he gathers data through observation or one-on-one interviews with open-ended questions. An interviewer can ask probing questions, taking the interview in many directions. It is likely that no two interviews with the same participant will produce the same answers. Although qualitative researchers strive to understand phenomena from their participant's perspective, they recognize that they also have a socially constructed worldview that affects how they conduct research (Creswell, 2013). For example, a tattoo enthusiast will approach research about tattooing differently than would a person who believed it to be a deviant activity. It is important, then, that researchers make clear their relationship to the phenomena being studied and examine their biases.

To carry out their research, students can choose from a daunting number of qualitative methodologies. The *Sage Encyclopedia of Qualitative Methods* lists nearly one hundred entries in their "approaches and methodologies" (Given, 2008). Creswell's (2013) text is welcomed in that it lists five traditions: ethnography, phenomenology, narrative, grounded theory, and case study. Johnson and Christensen (2013) also identify five approaches, but replace narrative inquiry with historical inquiry. Asking why there are so many qualitative approaches is akin to asking painters why they needs so many brushes. Each methodology, like each brush, is used to make a specific mark. In the section that follows, I will briefly describe the five approaches outlined by Creswell and the methods used to collect data.

Ethnography

Ethnography developed from anthropology as a method of gathering data enabling researchers to describe a cultural group. Ethnography refers to both the written description of the group and the methodological approach used to gain a perspective of what it is like to be a member (Johnson & Christensen, 2013). Ethnographers strive to understand the culture from an *emic*, or insider, point of view. To conduct fieldwork, researchers travel to and live with cultural groups for extended periods of time. Originally, these cultural groups were non-Western and viewed as exotic by the researchers and their readers. Today culture can mean, for example, a group of men living in a homeless shelter in Paris or a group of five years olds going to school for the first time in Pittsburgh.

Ethnographic methods rely on participant observation and interviews, methods that require researchers to be involved with their participants and be immersed in the culture they are studying for a prolonged period of time. For example, a researcher studying kindergarten-aged children might need to spend an entire school year observing a class. This allows the researcher to see an entire cycle and to observe the various rituals from the first day to the end of the year. The researcher must take time to gain entry into the culture to be studied and to become immersed in their daily lives. They will need to establish a rapport with members of the culture and likely interview key people from the culture. These methods produce data that allow researchers to write accurately about the culture they have studied.

Phenomenology

Phenomenology is the study of how people experience a phenomenon and how they interpret that experience. Like ethnography, the researcher attempts to understand the experience from his or her participants' point of view. For van Manen (1997), a key proponent of the methodology,

> To know the world is profoundly to be in the world a certain way, the act of researching—questioning—theorizing is the intentional act of attaching ourselves to the world, and which brings the world into being for us and in us. Then research is a caring act. (p. 5)

Professions, such as nursing, that focus on care and empathy find the methodology attractive (Johnson & Christensen, 2013). Phenomenology values other people's experiences, such as how people experience pain, grief, or happiness. A typical research question asks, "What is it like to experience…?"

Researchers gather data through interviews, journals, diaries, drawings and art, and observation. Phenomenology is deeply embedded in the philosophy of Husserl, Heidegger, Merleau-Ponty and others (Creswell, 2013). I agree with Creswell who recommends that students planning to take this approach should have an in-depth understanding of the philosophical assumptions of phenomenology.

Narrative Research

Narrative research involves studying the lives of individuals through the stories they tell (Creswell, 2013). Knowledge is created through listening to and shaping experience. For Chase (2011), narrative research begins with a "famous trilogy – biography, history, and society" (p. 421). The researcher gathers stories through extended interviews, then "restories" the data in a narrative chronology. In this way, researchers collaborate with the participant to create the final text. Johnson and Christensen (2013) expand narrative research to include places or events in the past and Tedlock (2011) adds to the list "history, drama, biography, autobiography, creative non-fiction, and narrative ethnography" (p. 335).

Johnson and Christensen (2013) use "historiography" to describe narrative research methods, writing, "Historiography involves the posing of questions, the collection of authentic source materials, the analysis and interpretation of those materials, and the composition of the results into a final report" (p. 50). In life history research, the participant is the authentic source and narrative researchers collect stories through in-depth interviews. The researcher can also draw on autobiographical writing, photographs, and other artifacts.

Creswell (2013) distinguishes between life history and oral history. Life history deals with individuals' entire lives and focuses on their understanding of how events have had a substantial impact on them. The accurate retelling of the event is not as important as the meaning the individual gives to the event in retelling it. An oral history, on the other hand, consists of personal reflections about events and their causes gathered from one individual or several individuals. Michael Hirsh's (2010) *The Liberators: America's Witnesses to the Holocaust,* in an example of oral history. Using the interview as his method, Hirsh collected 130 testimonies from service men and women who helped liberate World War II concentration camps. There are a number of digital oral history archives on events such as September 11 and Hurricane Katrina, available online (Janesick, 2015). Both life history and oral history research are valuable because researchers create a historical record of important events for future generations.

Grounded Theory

Grounded theory is an approach to generating and discovering a theory from data that has been systematically collected and analyzed (Johnson & Christensen, 2013). A theory is an explanation of how and why something operates. Glaser and Strauss first introduced the methodology in 1967. At the time, it was groundbreaking because it offered an alternative to the scientific method. Whereas the scientific method begins with a hypothesis to be tested, theory emerges from the data (Charmaz, 2006).

Grounded theory involves methods to collect the data and a systemic method to code the data. Like other qualitative methodologies, grounded study methods include interviewing, participant observation, and collecting and examining artifacts and texts. A unique feature of grounded study is that data collection and analysis are done concurrently using a constant comparison method (Charmaz, 2006; Dunne, 2011). A key characteristic of grounded theory is theory building (Urquhart, 2013).

Constant comparison is the process of comparing instances found in new data with what the researcher previously labeled as belonging to a certain category, and noting if the data are comparable (Urquhart, 2013). It also involves moving back and forth between data collection and analysis using various phases of coding. Urquhart, writing primarily for graduate students, suggests open coding, selective coding, and theoretical coding. She devotes a chapter to defining and providing examples of the open and selective coding, using terms like "stumbling blocks" and "terror" that students face when challenged with coding (p. 79). She allocates a chapter to the most important stage of coding, the theoretical phase.

The research methodology determines the form and level of engagement with existing literature at the proposal stage. Most studies require researchers to generate a hypothesis prior to collecting data and require extensive literature reviews, but when to conduct a literature review is a matter of dispute among those who use grounded theory methods (Charmaz, 2006). Glaser and Strauss (1967) advised against any review of literature at the beginning of the research process, holding that literature might bias the researcher or prevent the researcher from considering theories that emerged from the data. For Glaser (1998), writing an extensive literature review before collecting data is not a good use of time because relevant literature is not known at the onset. Many graduate students might welcome grounded theory as an opportunity to avoid an exhaustive literature review. However, Dunne (2011), whose doctoral thesis relied on grounded theory, views the literature review in practical terms in that it helped her articulate her research questions and justify her study (p. 121). Being aware of the research context can address some of the student's anxieties, and an early review is a necessary and important part of the research process.

Case Study

A case study can be about a single person, an institution, a department, or an event. The inquiry emphasizes depth over breadth. Case study research can be qualitative or qualitative, and is defined by the case, not the method. Yin (2009) recommends using case study research to answer a "how" or "why" question; and "when the investigator has little control over events;

and when the focus is on a current, real life context" (p. 2). For Simons (2015), case study differs from other qualitative research methods in that, "the purpose is to portray an in-depth view of the quality and complexity of social and educational programs or policies as they are implemented in specific socio-political contexts" (p. 458). Not all agree that the case study is a methodology. Others regard it as a choice of what to study or as an approach to research (Simons, 2015).

Choosing among the Methods

Qualitative research may use methods that seem similar and how they differ from each other may be unclear to students. Carter and Little (2007) provide clarity by describing a hypothetical student who wishes to study school-aged smokers. If the student studied the phenomena as an ethnographer, she would study the culture of smokers to "map and explain the 'smoking groups' at one or more schools as cultures or the culture of a particular school and the place of smoking within it" (p. 1323). As a phenomenological study, she would

> ... seek to uncover the essence or meaning of the smoking experience for the individual school-age people. A narrative-based methodology would guide her to ask about smoking in the life history of individual children. If she adopted grounded theory, she would set out to develop a substantive theory of school aged smoking. (p. 1323)

In all methodologies, she would use interview or observation methods and her final thesis would involve a detailed description of her findings.

Criteria for Judgment for Qualitative Research

Judging the quality of research has long vexed qualitative researchers and to date, there is no consensus. There are three perspectives on judging quality. First, some apply quantitative terms (internal validity, external validity, reliability, and objectivity) to qualitative research (Creswell, 2013). Others adopted alternative terms, such as Lincoln and Guba's (1985) notion of trustworthiness as an alternative to validity. For a study to be trustworthy, the researcher must establish its credibility, transferability, dependability, and confirmability (Rolfe, 2006). We say a study is credible when the researcher's interpretation corresponds to a participant's view of reality. A study's findings are transferable when they resonate with similar situations. Dependability relates addresses accuracy and consistency. Dependability somewhat relates to notions of reliability, but some hold that reliability has no relevance in qualitative research and we should not expect another researcher to arrive at the same categories (Rolfe, 2006). However, in qualitative research dependability means that the researcher is careful to collect and report the data collected. A study is confirmable when the data supports the researcher's claims. It corresponds to objectivity, in that the researcher is reflexive and transparent.

Although Lincoln and Guba's categories have remained the standard for 40 years, not all have agreed with adopting a framework borrowed from quantitative research. More recently, researchers regard reflexivity as important, recognizing the impossibility of remaining neutral, objective, and distant from their participants (Wheeldon & Ahlberg, 2012). Being reflective calls for researchers to critically examine how they shape their research and report their findings (Charmaz, 2006). Lincoln, Lynham, and Guba (2011) now regard validity as the ethical relationship researchers develop and maintain with their participants. They posit that validity is synonymous with authenticity. For Creswell (2013), validity is the accuracy of the findings, which come from spending adequate time with the participants.

Student Challenges

Qualitative research requires a considerable investment of time. Most ethnographic studies necessitate students relocating or residing in the field for a period of time. This time is extended by the need to first establish a rapport with members of the group. Oral history and life history research involves an investment of time to gather the stories from one or more participants. Narrative inquiry methods include in-depth interviews that take intensive interaction with the participants. For students who can invest the time to conduct a thorough study, qualitative research can be deeply rewarding. They provide the means for participants to tell stories that can deeply affect our understandings of them.

ACTION RESEARCH

Action research has been called a methodology, a method, a technique, a set of practices, and professional development (Clausen, 2012). It is under the umbrella of qualitative research, but its goals and actions set it apart from the previously described methodologies. Action research is used to find solutions to practical problems. As a methodology, it generates knowledge that is useful to the people who need it and who will put it to use. The primary goal of all action researchers is to spark change (McNiff, 2013). The researcher does not strive for objectivity nor take a disinterested stance to the research. They actively work to bring about positive solutions. Action researchers must continually examine their biases and consider how they affect all aspects of the research. Action research can be carried out by individuals or by people working together to improve their practice. As such, this methodology is particularly suited for those who work in educational and health care fields.

Kurt Lewin (1946) pioneered action research. He worked in industrial and organizational settings and advocated for a scholarship that was purposeful and engaged, writing, "Research that produces nothing but books will not suffice" (p. 37). Lewin, whose research addressed problems of segregation and discrimination, developed the spiral model used by most action researchers. This involves planning, fact-finding, and execution, which evolved into the action-reflection cycle of planning, acting, observing, and reflecting (McNiff, 2013).

Herr and Anderson (2015) list nearly twenty terms used to describe action research approaches, among them participatory action research (PAR), youth participatory action research (YPAR), practitioner research, and self-study. While there are nuances about key issues of each form, most insist, "inquiry is done *by* or *with* insiders of an organization or community, but never *to* or *on* them" (Herr & Anderson, 2015, p. 3).

Participatory Action Research (PAR) is a specific application of action research and carries with the imperative to impart social change (MacDonald, 2012). It is informed by the theories of Paulo Freire, who studied adult literacy. Researchers who adopt PAR as their method challenge the traditional hierarchies and power inherent in research relationships by seeking full collaboration of all participants and are committed to the "radical transformation of social reality and improvement in the lives of the individuals involved" (MacDonald, 2012, p. 39).

As a methodology, PAR is unique in that members of community, not the researcher, identify the problem or research question and are active co-researchers, involved in every aspect of the research process. They collect and analyze data and determine how and where it will be presented (MacDonald, 2012). This requires active involvement of the community at all levels of the research. PAR generally involves groups that are oppressed by and marginalized from mainstream society for political, economic, and other reasons. PAR researchers help individuals become more self-reliant by making them aware of their own resources. In addition, "PAR allows the researcher to be a committed participant, facilitator, and learner in the research process, which fosters militancy, rather than detachment"

(MacDonald, 2012, p. 39). A PAR researcher's agenda is one of advocacy, committed to give voice to those who are vulnerable, powerless, or silenced in society.

Youth Par (YPAR) maintains the same values as PAR, and is conducted by youth, both in schools and community settings (Herr & Anderson, 2015). YPAR allows young people to investigate topics that are meaningful to themselves, uncover the root causes of the problem, and to take action to influence policy makers to make changes. The researcher's goal is to teach youth that society's injustices are produced and can be challenged. An important characteristic of all participatory inquiry is that researchers and participants are considered to be equals who share the power that comes from being researchers. When enacting YPAR methodologies, researchers must negotiate the unequal power structures inherent in adult/youth relationships. Many PAR researchers hold positions of authority over the youth, such as teachers and program directors. For YPAR to be effective, the issues must address the concerns of the youth.

Given the difficulty of locating a group and working closely with its members, it is understandable that some researchers turn the lens on themselves. Self-study employs action research when researchers use the spiral approach to examine their own practice to make a change. Self-study involves "identifying an issue, collecting baseline data, implementing a plan and documenting and reflecting our present actions in order to revise our future actions" (Kitchen & Stevens, 2005, p. 2). The approach mirrors teaching practice and is useful for teachers and those who prepare students to become teachers.

Action researchers employ similar methods to qualitative researchers. Among them are focus groups interviews, participant observation, and interviews (MacDonald, 2012). Those conducting self-study may also collect data from journals, email correspondence, lesson plans, and written reflections (Kitchen & Stevens, 2005).

Student Challenges

Herr and Anderson (2015) bookend their student dissertation guide with stories about the lack of support they encountered at their universities. They conclude with the warning, "The action research dissertation is not for everyone. For those who have a low tolerance for ambiguity and messiness, action research would probably not be the best path taken" (p. 161). What does "messiness" mean for the student action researcher?

Although the spiral of plan, act, and reflect provides researchers with precise steps to follow, the research itself can feel like it is spiraling out of control. The components overlap and loop back. Reflection does not start and stop with the next iteration. Teasing apart the strands to write the report is not easy. The researcher should anticipate conflicts with some participants over interpretation and analysis of the data. There is a shared ownership of the research and researchers must negotiate its use. The goals of the academic, which are to publish and present the research findings, may be in sharp contrast to the goals of the participants.

Action research can require more time than other methodologies and students on strict timelines should take this into consideration. It takes time to establish rapport and build trust. Students who wish to conduct PAR must first identify a community with which they will work, and allow time for members to collectively generate the question or identify the problem they wish to pursue. MacDonald (2012) notes that researchers must gain access into communities, which can be challenging if the researcher is not from the community or is from a different background. Communities are not heterogeneous groups of individuals who agree with each other. Action research means a greater involvement with the community and this gives rise to the potential for conflicts that may impact the thesis process. It can be difficult to keep participants, especially youth, involved in the research. This is often the case for research that unfolds over time.

Those conducting action research may be disappointed when there is no improvement despite their best efforts. Some plans work, but others fail. For many, there is no great epiphany or defining moment of transformation.

Action research can be in tension with academic regulations. Students may have difficulty writing and getting a proposal accepted because the research is emergent. Each new plan is based on the previous iteration and cannot be anticipated in advance of the research. It may also be difficult to obtain ethics approval. To conduct PAR, researchers need to spend time with the community, but many ethics guidelines do not allow recruitment to begin before approval. This is discussed in greater detail in the following chapter.

PAR does not always conform to thesis guidelines. For example, a doctoral student wanted to include a co-authored chapter in her thesis, but her program required the thesis be solely authored by the student. She reluctantly claimed sole authorship of work that was collaboratively created.

Some dismiss action research as professional development or an attempt to do social work without training in the field. Levin and Greenwood (2011) write, "To many social scientists, action research is 'mere activism' and is viewed as a retreat from rigorous theories and methods" (p. 29). This can affect future employment in the academy and may make it difficult for students to publish and apply for funding. However, there are a number of journals that publish action research, so the possibility of publication is available.

Why Do Action Research?

With these limitations, why would anyone want to conduct action research? The attrition rate for Ph.D. students in social sciences is high, but few students drop out because they are incapable of doing graduate work. They drop out for other reasons. To complete a graduate degree, the odds must be in a student's favor. He or she needs a supportive supervisor, organizational and writing skills, knowledge of how to apply a method, and time to devote to reading and writing. Most of all, he or she needs motivation. Students who pursue action research have a passion to make a difference in people's lives, and their passion transcends the degree requirement. They echo Kurt Lewin in their conviction that "Research that produces nothing but books will not suffice" (p. 37).

ARTS METHODOLOGIES AND METHODS

Riddett-Moore and Siegesmund (2012) posit that arts-based research began when social scientists accepted the camera as a means for producing valid data. Early ethnographers regarded photographs as truthful witnesses to the scenes they portrayed. As methods, the arts have been used to elicit and describe data, and at times, to replace written texts. More recently, creative practice is being theorized as a way of knowing. The epistemological discussions are ongoing as theorists grapple with questions of how art produces knowledge and how we access artistic ways of knowing. This section addresses the many questions students have when considering arts research. What questions can it answer? What methods are used for arts-based research? How does one judge its quality? How does a doctoral student demonstrate an arts-based thesis contributes to knowledge?

There is a flurry of excitement about the potentials of arts research, and a plethora of names used to brand it. The many authors who contributed to Knowles and Cole (2008) *Handbook of the Arts in Qualitative Research: Perspectives, Methodologies, Examples, and Issues* use a myriad of terms, including arts informed research, image based research, art-as-research, arts-based research in education (ABER), and A/R/Tography, among others.

Chilton and Leavy's (2015) "partial lexicology" includes 27 terms for arts-based research. The terms are often used interchangeably and without definition.

One approach to understanding arts research is to tease apart Riddett-Moore and Siegesmund's (2012) three manifestations of art research: as a therapeutic intervention, as social science, and as studio practice. Admittedly, there are more categories, and each division may seem further afield. Isolating the stands can help students make decisions about the type of research best suited for their research.

As Art Therapy

The American Art Therapy Association (2013) explains that art therapy can entail helping clients explore feelings, deal with conflicts and addictions, reduce anxiety and stress, and increase self-esteem. Art therapy and creative arts therapy make use a number of art forms, such as the visual arts, music, dance and drama, combining artistic expression with various therapeutic approaches. Art therapists encourage their clients to engage in art making. McNiff (2008) applied approaches often used in art therapy to his research, defining art-based research as "the systematic use of the artistic process…as a way of understanding and examining experience by both researchers and the people they involve in their research" (p. 29).

Leavy (2015) notes that, "praxis is the doing of research—the *practice* of research" (p. 3). What constitutes the praxis of art research? An example of art research using art therapies comes from Snow, Snow, and D'Amico (2008) who directed a musical ethno-drama representing the everyday reality of 18 individuals with developmental disabilities. Snow et al. (2008) integrated data from interviews and focus groups with music, drama, dance, and playback theatre to change audience members' perceptions of people with developmental disabilities and to effect therapeutic change for the performers.

As Social Science Research

According to Chilton and Leavy (2015) arts-based research began in the 1970s, and quickly captured the attention of those conducting research in the social science fields. For Barone and Eisner (2012), "Arts-based research is, at its deepest level, about artistic and aesthetic approaches to raising and addressing social issues" (p. 57). Barone and Eisner (2012) make a clear distinction between arts-based research and artistic research (described in the following section). They view the two forms of research as existing on opposite ends of a research continuum, one being science and the other "high art" (p. 24). Arts-based research is used widely in nursing, education sociology, and communication studies. Social scientists advocate the use of arts to express ways of knowing that cannot be articulated by language. The cliché, a picture is worth a thousand words, supports the notion that art and images can be powerful means of communication. Art is not used to illustrate the findings, but rather to provide a greater meaning of the findings. Research can rely on a number of genres, including poetry, dance, performance, fiction, and visual arts (Chilton & Leavy, 2015).

Photography in particular has been used extensively in social science research (Holm, 2015). Photographs are used to elicit data in interviews and to aid in memory work in life history research. The images can be pre-existing, such as family albums, or generated by participants who create images as part of the research process. Photography is easier to use than other art forms, because most adults lack the graphic skills to effectively communicate through activities such as drawing and painting. For his master's thesis, MacLeod (2013) used photographs taken from family albums to aid in memory and evoke stories of a predominately Irish Canadian neighborhood that was in the process of being razed to make room to build condos. During his interviews, MacLeod asked participants to stand in the place where the original photograph was taken and recall memories about the moments when the photograph was taken. His thesis demonstrates the power photographs have to evoke rich and detailed memories.

As Studio Art Practice

Practice lead research, research-creation, practice as research, and studio based inquiry are a few of the terms used to describe, and in many cases, legitimize, what artists have done for centuries (Chapman & Sawchuk, 2012; Manning, 2015; Vaughan, 2005). Manning claims research-creation started as a funding category for artists who did not have the requisite Ph.D.s to obtain large academic grants. Studio inquiry is the subject of lively theoretical discussions and at the heart of the debate are questions of how the arts can generate knowledge.

Vaughan's engagement with collage provides an example of research-creation. Collage uses existing images, photographs, and materials to create a new image (Vaughan, 2005). Vaughan uses her father's childhood photograph album, containing 277 photographs to inform five textile sculptures that reveal her father's history and her complex relationship to him. She designed the garments not intended to be worn, but rather to signify an absent body, reflective of his absence during her childhood. In her work, *Unwearable: Parka*, Vaughan makes "an evocative representation of [her] father and others—perhaps of his race, class, gender, location, and time" (p. 14).

How Does One Judge the Quality of Arts Research?

Although the use of art in social science research is gaining acceptance, arts-based researchers face some challenges. As an emerging method of research, arts-based research has been embraced for its possibilities to disrupt research, but criticized as being neither credible research nor good art. Critics dismiss arts-based research for being less rigorous than other more established qualitative methodologies. Peers may challenge arts-based researchers who perform their findings as dance or poems by asking if what they are doing is indeed research. Chenail (2008) notes, "If that query is offered, invariably someone else will make the observation, 'So what!'" (p. 7). Arts-based researchers are fighting the same battles for legitimacy that qualitative researchers fought decades earlier.

On the other front, some artists criticize arts-based researchers as not being good artists. Piirto (2002), a scholar and poet, asks how much must someone study his or her art before writing a dissertation or a peer-reviewed paper. She answers her own question by stating, "Let us welcome our artist-educators, as well as our self-exploring novices. But let us not confuse the quality of their qualifications for rendering, making marks, embodying, and distilling. Let us not confuse the seekers for the masters" (p. 444). Academics are territorial and attack those who are seen to encroach on their terrain. Some artists, who spend their careers honing artistic skills, resent the newcomers.

Artists who engage in research-creation are not confronted with similar attacks because they are entrenched deeply in their own territory. The art world has long established protocols for critiquing art. Granting agencies and galleries elevate some artists while ignoring others. Artists know that notions of quality are relative, and art works that are scorned today can become part of tomorrow's canon. How, then, does one judge art research? Importantly, how can doctoral students demonstrate their arts-based or research-creation theses contribute to knowledge?

A number of researchers are working independently to establish criteria for judging art research (Barone & Eisner, 2012; Lafrenière & Cox, 2012; Leavy, 2015; Manning, 2015). For Manning, "New processes will likely create new forms of knowledge which may have no means of evaluation within current disciplinary models" (p. 53). Barone and Eisner (2012) suggest general terms to provide some guidance. They include incisiveness, concision, coherence, generativity, social significance, and evocation and illumination (p. 148). Research is incisive when it addresses a specific social issue and answers the critic's "So what?" question. Concision, as it relates to art making, means that only what is needed should appear, nothing more. A haiku is a concise form of poetry. Coherence refers to the quality of the art form. A novel must adhere to the literary style and the story should hold together. Generativity refers to a work's ability to reach beyond the maker and speak to a larger issue. Vaughan's work, though deeply personal, speaks to men of a certain social class parenting in the early 1960s. Social significance addresses the need to contribute to society, as did the work of Snow et al. (2008). It requires art researchers to address social issues in order to improve lives for others. MacLeod's work addresses the plight of families who are displaced through the gentrification of their neighbors. Evocation and illumination mean the audiences should be emotionally moved by the art. For a thesis, the work must not only be original, but it should contribute in a substantial way to the field. Additionally, in Chilton and Leavy's (2015) terms, it should have "aesthetic power" (p. 415). Lafrenière and Cox add that art research "must have an appreciable effect on the audience's understanding of or appreciation for the studies finding" (p. 322).

Leavy (2009), Baron and Eisner (2012), and others support the notion that research can be both credible and fictional. Lafrenière and Cox, however, do not endorse fiction within research because it does not relate to the criteria of research. I believe that there are times a researcher must write fiction in order to tell the truth. Ethics and social responsibility can cause researchers to omit that which is truthful, but can cause harm. For Leavy (2013), fictional characters and events emerge from research with the hopes of portraying real and authentic lives. Researchers incorporate empirical details that resonate as truthful to sensitively portray characters.

Why Conduct Art Research

This question has been eloquently answered by Vaughan (2005):

> To embed my own work more deeply in the experimental tenor of these times, to work toward ensuring that more of us appreciate what art knows and to find ways to explore and represent that knowledge, and to find personally appropriate ways to work with the arts' emancipatory potential and effect social change. (p. 16)

The arts can bring pleasure and a sense of wonder to research. This does not make the research less rigorous, but it can make research more fun and meaningful for the researcher and the participants.

WRITING THE METHODOLOGY SECTION OR CHAPTER

The methodology section, whether for a proposal or the final thesis, begins by defending the methodology as providing the best answer to the research question. Students need to determine what knowledge is needed to answer their question. We return to the nesting dolls metaphor and consider how the epistemology, the methodology, the methods used to collect data, and the procedure fit together to form the methodology chapter.

The question suggests the methodology. Students who know their methodology well and understand its values, its history, and its limitations will encounter fewer problems when attempting to put it into practice and later defend the evidence they gathered. Students may be excited to use a specific methodology but later find it did not allow them to answer their questions. Or, the desire to answer a specific question can be at odds with the student's resources and skills. The question and the approach to the answer should be a comfortable fit. Does the question suggest a quantitative or qualitative approach? If quantitative, does it require experimental, quasi-experimental, or a descriptive methodology? If qualitative, which methodology best answers the question?

Next, consider the methods that will be used to collect data. This section needs a greater discussion than simply naming the tool. For example, students who want to interview participants must consider the numerous methods used to conduct interviews. A focus-group interview will yield a different data set than will a one-on-one interview. Interview methods involve more than asking a participant questions. Other instruments the student intends to use to gather data should be fully discussed. For example, if a study uses a questionnaire, was it used in other studies? Has it been validated? If the student modifies the questionnaire, they should describe the reason for the changes and the steps taken to validate it. Students are advised to locate and follow a guide for each selected method. The guide will suggest the procedures to systematically obtain data. It is not wise to take an ad hoc approach to using methods. Messy is one thing. Squalor is another. Data collected in a haphazard manner is much harder to analyze and use to draw convincing conclusions.

The procedure section describes the exact steps that will be taken for the research and identifies how the methods will be applied. It answers who, what, where, and how questions. Who are the participants? How will they be recruited? How many are needed for the study? What will they be asked to do? Where will the study take place? What is the research design? The procedure section should take the reader logically through the steps of the research. The procedures should take into account how the data will be analyzed and any ethical considerations. Some disciplines include a discussion of the study's limitations.

The research procedures should be in harmony with any ethical considerations. The ethical guidelines determine how participants will be treated throughout the study. They determine the levels of privacy and their rights for voluntary participation. This issue is taken up in greater detail in the following chapter.

The methodology chapter also includes a detailed plan for analyzing the data. Admittedly, some methodologies allow for data to emerge and students cannot know the exact nature of the data at the outset of the research. However, the more time students spend anticipating what the data might consist of and how it will be analyzed before collecting, the fewer problems they will encounter later. Chapter 8 provides a greater discussion of ways to code qualitative data.

The limitation section should include a discussion of the study's parameters and factors over which students have no control. For example, the study on teenage cultural practices may include females only. Limits include the three constraints listed by Single (2010): "resources, time, and knowledge" (p. 24). Some students, wanting to generalize from a qualitative study, view the focus on small, local contexts as a limitation. To minimize this limitation, they collect large amounts of data to generalize and when analyzing it, find themselves to be drowning in the data. This is not a limitation, but rather, the wrong use of a methodology.

There are times when opportunities allow students to collect data before they have articulated a question and written a proposal. Although these offers are tempting, students should be aware that it is difficult to map data gathered in an ad hoc fashion onto a systematic methodology. And, as will be discussed in the next chapter, retroactive ethics approval is discouraged because participants were not afforded their rights of informed consent and right to withdraw. This last constraint brings us to the importance of the topic of the next chapter: ethical research.

CONDUCTING ETHICAL RESEARCH

INTRODUCTION

Conducting research involves risks. Most risks are minor but others can be life altering for both researchers and those who participate in our research. It is imperative that as researchers, we weigh the social benefits of our study against any potential harm we may cause. Students who involve others in their research must comply with university ethical procedures. To write this chapter, I consulted governmental policy statements, reviewed literature, and discussed ethical issues with my university's ethics compliance officer. However, ethical decisions rely on judgment and specific universities and departments interpret and apply policies in many ways. One university's ethics review board might grant unconditional approval, while another rejects the same proposal. Research ethics are discipline and context specific. This chapter provides suggestions on how to obtain ethics approval, but should not be viewed as a legal authority on the subject. All questions and concerns should be addressed first by the student's supervisor, who has likely navigated the ethics procedure for his or her own research.

Many students fear and loathe the ethics approval process. Indeed, the process can be a time-consuming venture that alters the researcher's original purpose and shapes how research is conducted. Most universities require that researchers secure ethics approval before any research activity can take place. Conducting research without ethics approval is a violation of academic codes of conduct. Although this rarely happens, students can be charged with academic misconduct if they begin their research without approval. In some cases, any data collected before receiving ethics approval cannot be used in the research or included in the thesis.

It is helpful to read and follow the university's ethics guidelines while writing the proposal, especially when determining the research methodology and procedures. The guidelines will help shape how participants are recruited and treated throughout the study. Most universities provide templates for submitting requests to the research ethics board and they only review requests submitted on proper forms. Become familiar with the template and its language. Students are advised to wait until their thesis committee approves their proposal before submitting requests to the university review board. If the thesis committee makes substantial changes to the research, the student may be required to submit a new request. Some research ethics boards require that members of the thesis committee approve in principle how the research will be conducted before allowing students to submit a formal request.

Not all research projects require ethics approval, but it is important to verify this with the university's office of research ethics before starting any recruitment or data collection. Students who conduct research under the auspices of their supervisor's research may not be required to obtain ethical approval, provided the supervisor previously obtained approval. However, it is a good idea to become familiar with the approval process for future research. If the compliance officer decides the research does not require ethics approval, it is advised to get this decision in writing in case any problems arise.

Attend workshops provided by the school of graduate studies or the office of ethics to demystify the approval process. Get to know those who work in the university's research ethics office. They can provide fast answers and suggest ways to phrase responses to the board's questions that make the review process faster and easier. More importantly, they can spot unintentional red flags that will cause concern among board members, slowing the approval process. They can inform students when the review boards meet to help plan submission timelines.

Who and What Govern the Ethics Policies and Procedures?

In the United States, the Department of Health and Human Service's (2009) *Code of Federal Regulations, Human Subjects Research* is charged with the protection of human subjects. The Canadian Institute of Health Research, Natural Science and Engineering Research Council of Canada, and Social Sciences and Humanities Research Council of Canada's (2014) *Tri-council policy statement: Ethical conduct for research involving humans* determines the guidelines and principles for research in Canada. Researchers must comply with all conditions to receive government funding for research. Both documents set out clearly defined rules for a peer-review process. In the United States, the review committee is called an institutional review board (IRB) and in Canada, the research ethics boards (REB). Nearly all research conducted in North America and the United Kingdom is subject to similar guidelines (Wiles, 2013). These guidelines define the number of faculty members making up the review board, which must be comprised of faculty members from various disciplines to ensure that proposals will be viewed from multiple perspectives.

What Power Do Research Ethics Boards Have?

University ethics review boards are responsible for reviewing ethics requests for their university community. They are appointed by their departments or faculties and serve a multi-year term. They are usually active researchers and familiar with the types of research they assess. Regular board meetings are held monthly throughout the academic year. Frequently, review boards do not meet during the summer, so it is advised that students submit requests early in the academic year.

Research ethics boards have the authority to approve, require modifications, or deny requests. Often, the board will comment on the request and point to areas that must be corrected or elaborated upon. This is referred to as "conditional status." Although the request has been given conditional approval, recruitment of participants and data collection cannot start until full approval is granted. Comments must to be addressed to the satisfaction of the board even if the researcher does not agree. Arguing with an ethics review board is futile. They will withhold approval, delaying the research process. Research ethics boards have a great deal of power to let researchers into the field or to keep them on the sidelines. Universities usually have procedures to appeal the decision of the review boards, but doing so takes time and energy, both better put toward the thesis research.

Navigating Human Subjects Research Protocol Forms

Standard research protocol forms often begin by asking the researcher to explain, in general terms, the purpose of the research. The researcher must clearly articulate the benefits of the research both to the participants and society as a whole, and indicate the level of risk it poses. Risk levels range from minimum to high, and include physical, psychological, financial, and social risks. As researchers, we must ask ourselves if our research can do harm to those who agree to act as participants. A study of gossip in a small town may be revealing, but what happens to individuals after the researcher leaves the community? What happens when people tell stories about each other? How and who does the research benefit? For many studies, there are no easy answers. As researchers, we are required to identify the risks and indicate what we will do to minimize their effects.

Research is deemed to have minimal risk when harm or discomfort is not more than that which one would encounter in everyday life and when participants are healthy adults over the age of 18. For example, Canada's Tri-Council Policy (2014) states that, "Observational research that does not allow for the identification of the participants in the dissemination of the results, that is not staged by the researcher, and is non-intrusive should normally be regarded as minimal risk" (p. 142). However, this research still requires approval from the research ethics board. The risk level indicated determines the intensity of scrutiny the request will be given.

Any research involving children or vulnerable populations is usually considered as high risk and students who plan to include child participants should anticipate greater levels of scrutiny and a longer review time. Research ethics boards question whether or not children can give informed consent. The standard consent form may need to be modified for children since additional consent is required from parents or guardians.

Researchers must describe the ways they will be recruiting participants and may be asked to provide samples of advertisements and recruitment letters. If recruiting in person, research ethics boards may ask for a verbatim script to ensure the researcher is not being deceptive. People who participate in studies must know and understand what will be asked of them throughout the research process.

Informed consent also means that participants must know that, at all times, they are the subjects of research and how and when the researcher is collecting data. Generally, they must be given information to permit them to know what the researcher is studying. However, informing people they are part of research can and does alter behavior. In some cases, deception or incomplete disclosure may be permitted, but the researcher must justify the use of deception and explain why it is necessary to achieve the goals of the study.

Deception can take many forms, some more covert than others. Deception means that participants are given false or inaccurate information, whereas incomplete disclosure means they are not given complete information about the purpose of the research. It can mean purposefully misleading people about the researcher's identity or being less than forthcoming about the reasons for the research. For example, a researcher who is conducting a field study in a small community may elect to attend church related activities when, normally, the researcher does not attend a church. Some researchers simply change how they dress in order to fit into the group they are studying. A researcher who normally wears a suit and tie may have difficulty establishing rapport with a graffiti crew. But, deception can cause problems, especially if the participants forget the researcher is collecting data. This is particularly an issue in ethnographic research or where gaining rapport is necessary to carry out the research. Over time, participants may forget they are research subjects and come to think of the researcher as a friend. They might confide in the researcher as a friend, forgetting that what they say may become public in a published paper or thesis.

Researchers deliberately using deception are required to describe debriefing sessions. During debriefing sessions, participants are given complete information about the goals and purpose of the research and told why it was necessary to deceive or withhold information from them. Research ethics boards may also ask that, after the debriefing session, participants be given the opportunity to withdraw their consent to participate or withdraw their data from the study.

Participating in research must be a voluntary act and participants have the right to withdraw from the research at any time. Instructions on how they go about doing this should be indicated on the consent form. Usually, participants may inform a third party that they wish to withdraw from the study. If participants are financially compensated for their participation, payment should be pro-rated throughout the research. Giving participants a lump sum payment at the study's conclusion may be viewed as coercion because if they withdraw, they will not be paid. Researchers cannot attempt to convince anyone to remain a participant.

Participants must know the level of privacy they will be given by the researcher. There are levels of confidentiality, ranging from fully identified to undisclosed. They may be given pseudonyms, for example. Participants who provide information must be informed of how and where their information will be published or presented.

Consent Forms

In addition to the protocol form, researchers must also create a consent form for participants to sign before conducting research. Again, most universities have available templates. The consent form should speak directly to the participant and include a description of what they will be asked to do and indicate the time commitment required. They must be informed of the degree to which the information they provide will be kept confidential. The form should include names and phone numbers of people they can contact should they have questions about the research or about their rights as a participant. Usually, this contact is the university's compliance office.

The consent form must include a statement that they can stop participating at any time. The consent form tells them what will happen to the data they provide. Will it be published? Will it be presented at conferences? Some universities also have templates for consent for research involving deception, which must be signed after debriefing sessions.

Multi-Jurisdiction Research

Increasingly, research is collaborative and can involve a number of sites, such as schools, prisons, hospitals, or other universities. Students should be informed about the approval process of each institution before writing a proposal or submitting an ethics request to their university. For example, a graduate student proposed to interview professors from universities across North America. After obtaining approval from her home university, she discovered she required approval by the research ethics board of each participant's university. Some institutions have a reciprocal review process and the university compliance office can provide information as to which universities have such protocols in place. Offsite approval can take up to a year, and requests may be denied with no opportunity for resubmission. Some charge fees for submitting requests, many of which are non-refundable if the request is denied. Many institutions have specific guidelines and policies for research activities that differ from that of the university.

METHODOLOGICAL CONSIDERATIONS

Action Research

Each methodology presents specific ethical challenges. This is especially the case for research that blurs the lines between professional practice and academic research. Researchers, in disciplines such as education, nursing, medicine, clinical psychology, and social work, occupy duel roles and may conduct research on or with individuals who also receive their care or instruction. Research ethics boards closely examine requests from practitioner-researchers to ensure the participants are volunteering for the research and that they are able to give informed consent to participate. Third party recruitment is necessary to ensure that participants provided voluntary consent to participate in the research and were not coerced.

As with all research, research ethics boards pay attention to the power dynamics between the researcher and the participant. It must be possible for a participant to withdraw from research activity, yet continue to receive full services. The third party should act as the designate contact person for participants who wish to withdraw from the research. Usually, the researcher should be unaware of who has and who has not agreed to participate in the study until the end of the relationship. For example, teachers who conduct action research should not know whether or not students have agreed to participate in their research until after the grades have been assigned and the course is over. This is usually accomplished by having a director or principal explain the research protocols to participants prior to the research and oversee the signing of consent forms. The participants should always know when the researcher is collecting data.

Ethics and Self-Reflective Research

Research that involves self-reflective methodologies, such as autoethnography, links the researcher's personal experiences to wider social and political issues. On the surface, it would seem that the ethics approval is not required because the researcher is the sole participant. At many universities, this is not the case. Autoethnographic research may require ethics approval if individuals other than the researcher can be identified in any written texts or oral presentations that result from the inquiry. These individuals are considered to be research participants and are entitled to the same rights as participants in any other research. Researchers must ensure that participants are given the opportunity to provide informed consent before the research begins and can determine their preferred level of confidentiality in presentations and publications.

Participants should be given the opportunity to read sections of the research that identifies them. Further, they should be given permission to remove any sections they deem to be harmful. Ellis (2007), a leading writer and practitioner of autoethnography, holds that it may not always be possible and such restrictions may silence researchers. She argues that, in some cases, social justice benefits outweigh the rights of individuals who may be harmed by being named in research. This point is echoed by Reilly (2013), who writes, "Sometimes as researchers we need to make a mess and create a fuss to highlight the pain and suffering, violence, injustice, and emotional wounding in the world" (p. 8). Ellis (2007) asks if the wellbeing of the researcher is less important than that of the participant. She cites an example of a student researcher who described abuse by a family member, and points out that giving the written account to that family member could cause her harm. On the other hand, Ellis cautions researchers who engage in autoethnography to "assume everyone in your story will read it" (p. 25). Further, she writes that she informs her students "that self-revelations always involved revelations about others. I tell them they don't own their story" (p. 24).

Tolich (2010) examined several published autoethnographic accounts paying particular attention to the potential harm the study might cause the researcher. Tolich cautions researchers to consider any consequence a confessional tale might have on their future careers. He advises researchers to regard their study "like an inked tattoo, posting an autoethnography to a Web site or making it part of a curriculum vitae, the marking is permanent" (p. 1608). Tolich's solution to minimize any harm to the researcher is to adopt a "nom de plume" (p. 1606), rather than give participants a pseudonym. However, this solution may not fit well with thesis requirements and career building.

INTERNET RESEARCH

The Internet is both a tool for research and a venue for research (Harriman & Patel, 2014). The Internet contains a wealth of data and the opportunity to recruit participants from all over the world. In many ways, Internet research ethics mirror that of traditional research. However, researching Internet culture can present researchers with unique ethical challenges.

Kitchin (2007) distinguishes between two types of web-based research: non-intrusive and engaged. Researchers use metaphors such as harvesting, capturing and data mining to describe non-intrusive research methods. Researchers might collect and analyze data already available on the Internet. This data may be drawn from blogs, public twitter feeds, and open online forums. This research involves no interaction and no intervention on the part of the researcher (Kozinets, 2015; Wiles, 2013,). The information collected was intended to be in the public domain and may be treated as published writing. In Kitchin's view, this type of research is not deemed to be human subject research, provided that no individual can be identified.

Kozinets (2015) coined the term "netnography" to describe a type of engaged social media research practice. Netnography uses data shared freely and not prompted or elicited by the researcher. However, researchers should consult the terms and conditions of the networking site to ascertain who owns the data they plan to harvest. Engaged research might involve collecting information in chat rooms and online forums. Ethics approval is required when membership is restricted and researchers are required to join or become a "friend," or seek access to role-play (Kitchin, 2007; Kozinets, 2015). Ethical concerns for ethnographic research should guide researchers in obtaining information from the Internet. Kozinets recommends disclosure when the researcher is a full participant.

Kitchin (2007) suggests that researchers obtain ethics approval for engaged research. She holds that collecting data from and about people on social networking sites should be treated as any other research involving humans. Individuals who participate in activities on the Internet are entitled to give or deny informed consent, to withdraw from the study, and to have privacy protection.

The Internet also offers possibilities for experimental research but may require special ethics consideration. Cornell University researchers, Kramer, Guillory, and Hancock (2014) conducted an experiment to test their hypothesis that "emotional states can be transferred to others via emotional contagion, leading people to experience the same emotions without their awareness" (p. 8788). The researchers randomly selected a sample of Facebook users (N=689,003) and manipulated the emotional content they received in their news feed. The news feed is the way users see what others have shared and according to the researchers, "Which content is shown or omitted in the News Feed is determined via a ranking algorithm that Facebook continually develops and tests in the interest of showing viewers the content they will find most relevant and engaging" (p. 8789). For one week in January 2012, the researchers altered the algorithms used to determine what appears in each individual's news feed. One group had their positive news reduced and the other group had their negative news reduced. Individuals in each group were then tracked to see if they were likely to submit positive or negative feeds.

After its publication, the research created a public outcry and brought ethical concerns of Internet research to the forefront (Harriman & Patel, 2014). The research was legal, but was it ethical? Facebook users had given consent to be part of research when they agreed to the terms of service to become a member. Facebook's Data Use Policy gives permission for "testing, research, and service improvement" (Verma, 2014, p. 10779). Users seldom read the lengthy agreement contracts provided by most social media sites. However, those selected for the experiment had no knowledge they had been selected nor had they been asked to give consent to participate. In addition they did not have the freedom to withdraw. However, we are subject to many low risk experiments. Kramer et al.'s study is not unlike the way a grocery store manager experiments with product placement by putting sweetened cereals at eye levels and oatmeal at the bottom of the shelf to entice shoppers to purchase the cereal.

Many research review boards are now developing guidelines for online research. Many require researchers to identify special safeguards to screen for children and vulnerable populations. Young people may recognize the risks associated with their online activities, but they may lack the knowledge and the skills to effectively deal with the risks (Wiles, 2013). One difficulty researchers encounter is assessing if participants are who they say they are, and identifying children who pose as adults.

Online Surveys

Internet surveys must allow individuals to give their informed consent to participate and to opt out of answering a question or stop taking the survey. Online surveys must protect people's identity, unless otherwise stated. Individuals who are asked to participate must be assured their participation is voluntary, that their privacy will be protected, and be assured they will be free of any psychological stress or harm (Wiles, 2013).

As journal editors, Harriman and Patel (2014) ask who is responsible for ethics approval of internet-based research. They ask if the ethics of one country apply to participants from another country. They point out that researchers may reside in a country with a policy that is different from the one found in their participants' country. They ask, "Does an ethics committee in one country have the jurisdiction to grant approval of a study that involves participants in another country?" (p. 2). Research ethics boards must determine what ethical guidelines researchers will need to adhere to when conducting international research.

The virtual world is a cultural space and researchers must adhere to the same ethical rules as in a non-virtual community. If data collection methods would raise eyebrows in the non-virtual environment, it will in the virtual world. Just as one would not lurk on a playground to observe children playing, one cannot do so online.

ETHICAL CONSIDERATION FOR CREATIVE RESEARCH PRACTICES

In 2008, a Social Sciences and Humanities Research Ethics Special Working Committee of Canada (SSHWC) formed to consider ethical guidelines for government funded artistic research (Blackstone et al., 2008). The committee attempted to find the balance between the free zone of anything goes and censorship, and called for universities to establish review boards specifically dedicated to artistic research. They called for decreasing the power of existing review boards to exercise restraint or censorship. Although Canada's Tri Council did not adopt the group's recommendations, the committee did make a number of insightful recommendations that are apropos here. First, the committee equated an exhibition to a scholarly presentation and, in doing so, eliminated the need for audience members to sign consent forms. We do not need to ask audience members in a presentation to give informed consent to hear a presentation. However, SSHWC drew a distinction between attending a performance as a spectator and being part of the research loop. The committee did not address any harm that viewing an artwork might cause an audience member and pointed out that risk was a highly prized aspect of the arts.

More recently, an interdisciplinary group of visual arts researchers working in Australia and Canada created *Guidelines for Ethical Visual Research Methods* (Cox, Drew, Guillemin, Howell, Warr, & Waycott, 2014). They identify six categories for ethical consideration: confidentiality, minimizing harm, consent, fuzzy boundaries, representation and audience, and authorship and ownership, (p. 8). For each consideration, the guidelines pose a number of thoughtful guiding questions for researchers and ethics approval boards to consider.

Confidentiality is similar to notions of the right of privacy in qualitative research, but visual methods may make it impossible to ensure complete anonymity. An example of a question is, "Is anonymity an appropriate strategy to maintain and protect confidentiality (for example blurring faces in photographs), or will alternatives need to be identified and agreed on?" (Cox et al., 2014, p. 10). Boydell et al. (2011) notes that "when preserving anonymity in work using photography, the standard method of blinding, which uses a black bar across the eyes to protect identity makes participants look unsavory or criminal, which exacerbates the potential for stigma and discrimination" (p. 9). The guidelines also ask researchers to consider different forms for different audiences, and notes that images created in one context may not be freely shared in another. This implicates methods where images are made in a community, but communities or individuals may not wish to exhibit outside of the community.

Minimizing harm is a concern for visual research methods in that harm is often unforeseen. Cox et al. (2014) provide the example of photo elicitation used to research sensitive topics positing, "evocative imagery, holds the danger that participants might suffer emotional harm from reliving upsetting events" (p. 11). They pose questions such as, "What harm might participants potentially encounter as a result of telling their stories through visual methods?" and "Will they expose participants to criticism/ridicule?" (p. 12). Also of concern is any potential harm for the viewers. "How should audience members be warned or protected when sharing imagery from visual methods that are potentially confronting?" (p. 12).

Consent is part of any research with humans, but Cox et al. (2014) ask researchers to consider that "it may be difficult for participants to fully understand the effects of producing images" (p. 12). Moreover, images do not always mean what the maker intended and can be read by audiences in many ways. Cox et al. suggest that consent is not a one-time event, but should be revisited throughout the research process. At times, consent should be revisited after the participant has lived with her or his decision.

Fuzzy boundaries refer to the blurring of roles in the research. It also means that the researcher is a co-creator in the artwork. Cox et al. recommend asking "Who is involved in the visual project, and what role/s do the different participants play?" (p. 17).

Ownership and authorship asks researchers to critically reflect on who owns the research and intellectual property. For example, who owns the photographs or a group quilt created as part of a community research study? Determining ownership is critical in academic research, where artist researchers must exhibit and present. Questions include, "What protocols are in place to generate, and sustain, a common understanding between researchers and participants around who owns images produced in the course of research, who can access them, and who is entitled to disseminate them?" (p. 19).

Similarly, representation and audience pertains to decisions about when and where the work will be shown. Researchers should ask, "Have appropriate consent and permission been sought from participants for representation and dissemination of visual research products?" (Cox et al., 2014, p. 20).

It is important to remember that these are guidelines not policies. Most researchers will have to adopt existing protocols and obtain approval for arts-based research.

COLLECTING AND ANALYZING DATA

COLLECTING DATA

Once ethics approval has been granted, and the supervisor and committee agree to the merits and feasibility of the proposed research, data collection can begin. Collecting the data, or actually doing the research, is the most exciting part of graduate school. However, even when armed with the best question and research design, things do not always go according to plan. This chapter begins with a discussion of the challenges students can encounter when collecting the data. It then turns its attention to methods of analyzing qualitative data collected. Yin (2009) notes, "Unlike statistical analysis, there are few fixed formulas or cookbook recipes to guide the novice" (p. 127). The chapter puts a greater focus on qualitative research because coding and analysis is interpretative and students are often on their own to make sense of the enormous quantity of data they have collected.

Recruiting and Retaining Participants

Students cannot recruit participants before obtaining ethics approval, so most operate on faith that others will be interested and willing to participate in their study. Many discover this is not the case and panic when recruitment ads bring fewer participants than expected or people do not take the time to answer even the most well crafted questionnaire. I advise students to be patient, and to widen the net. They may have specific participants in mind for the study, but others may provide equally valuable data.

Most students, at some point during their study, learn that they are more invested in their research than are their participants. Participants may start the research with excitement, but their interest may wane as time goes on. The thesis is not the participants' main concern, even in PAR, which is intended to benefit them and their community. They may embrace the action phase of research, but lose motivation when it comes time to analyze the data. A doctoral student who worked with several colleagues to conduct action research to "green" their curriculum discovered this. Her colleagues were fully engaged during the development and implementation phases, but were not involved in the reflection and data analysis. One teacher made this point clearly, stating, "This is your thesis, not mine." This point is well taken. While the ultimate goal of the graduate student is to produce a thesis, it is not the goal of the participants, nor do they have any responsibility to ensure one is produced.

Participants can drift in and out of a study, or drop out altogether. This is not the same as withdrawing, in which a participant makes a conscious choice to not be part of a study. Participants may leave for personal reasons, some unrelated to the research. Usually, researchers can use data collected from participants who drop out and that data can be very useful.

Dealing with Unanticipated Ethical Issues

Although university ethics approval protocols attempt to address issues such as "heinous discovery," "deception," and "right to withdraw," once researchers are in the field collecting data, ethical issues emerge. Problems are more prolific when dealing with other people's lives and stories. Students find themselves confronted with issues that were never covered in their methods courses. Many post-thesis publications posit, "No one told me this would happen" or "what I wish I knew before I started this research." Researchers cannot anticipate what will happen, and these papers attest to the transforming power of research.

Simply being in the field raises questions of identity. How do researchers present themselves? How does the researcher's appearance impact the research? Does one try to blend in, and appear like an undercover policeman? Identity goes beyond appearance and is concerned with the researcher's actions. For example, should a researcher go out for drinks with participants?

Money is at the root of some ethical issues. Students often view themselves as poor in society, and for good reason. Many are living below the poverty line, but this is a temporary (we hope) situation. However, compared to some of their participants, graduate students may be viewed as financially well off. Should the researcher reimburse participants for their time? Many university ethics offices may have guidelines concerning this, but they do not cover all possibilities. For example, should a researcher take participants places by car? Pick up the tab for groceries? Buy cigarettes and alcohol? Pay for lunch during an interview? Participants, too, can feel that the research is costing them. They may feel a responsibility to provide food and accommodations for the researcher, which can come at the expense of the needs of their family.

Many times researchers are given relevant information but revealing this information may have major consequences for the participant or the community. Orb, Eisenhauer, and Wynaden (2001) recount a story about a participant who revealed to a graduate student during an interview that she was involved in drug dealings. They point out: "The student was advised by one of the supervisors to delete the interview. A year later the participant's spouse was dead from drug abuse" (p. 94). Do researchers have the right to tell stories that can harm individuals or communities? Is it the researcher's responsibility to report hearsay evidence to authorities? Participants and the researcher need to be clear about what happens to data, where and how the data will be retold and reported before the interview begins, and after it concludes. Researchers may observe behaviors and situations they later decide to leave out of their thesis to avoid betraying the people who have opened their homes and communities to them. However, once the data is collected, most researchers feel obligated to use it. They have traveled to research sites, listened to the stories of others, written copious field notes, and collected images, all with the intention to use this data. Some may feel a responsibility to tell the stories of those who gave of their time to share them.

Rapport can develop into a friendship that blurs the role between researchers and members of the group they are researching. Ellis's (2007) widely criticized doctoral ethnography, *Fisher Folk*, provides an example. She writes of her experience and offers valuable insights to her students by distinguishing between being friendly and being friends with the participants. Being a friendly researcher yields different data than being a friend. Being a friend means researchers will be told stories in confidence, and they must grapple with the decision of whether or not to retell the story. When writing the data, the researcher cannot switch from being a friend to being a truthful observer. This was the case for Ellis, who wrote, "The people of Fishneck had forgotten and thought it was just 'Caroline, a friend, coming to visit'" (p. 7). However,

> When I returned to Fishneck, my friends confronted me with the words I had written: they reacted strongly to my descriptions of their smelling like fish, taking infrequent baths, being overweight, making little money, wearing mismatched clothing, having sex at an early age, and being uneducated. (p. 11)

Ellis (2007) can be faulted for crossing the professional line to be friends to collect data, and then crossing back to write her thesis. But, there is much tension between being a researcher and a friend, and I suspect many researchers agree with Ellis when she writes, "I felt I owed my readers the 'truth' and that my book served a greater good and larger purpose of understanding and disseminating knowledge" (p. 10). Ellis now contends that the participants, whether they are subjects or co-researchers, must know at all times when the researcher is collecting data. It is the researcher's responsibility to remind them of this. The issues and boundaries between friend and researcher are exacerbated by research that involves prolonged time with participants and multiple interviews.

What happens after the researcher leaves a research site? Ideally, the people who remain should be better off than before. At a minimum, they should be the same, so that a community might accept another researcher. Students should see research in the long-term, one where they will be invited back after they write and publish their research findings. If people feel used, it doesn't matter that knowledge was furthered for the field. To borrow a filmmaker's term, they have "burned a site."

Wiles (2013) distinguishes between ethical decisions made on moral principles and those made "on the basis of care, compassion and the desire to act in ways that benefit the individual or group who are the focus of the research" (p. 15). Reilly (2013) reflected on her research that examined how trauma impacts a community, and asks, "What do you do when the research you are conducting can both help and harm individuals or a community? Or, more specifically, harm one individual?" (p. 5). Reilly (2013) regards research as an "act of love" (p. 9) and Luttrell (2000) advises that researchers must find ways to both make realistic claims about their participants and honor their dignity. As Ellis (2007) tells her students, "People never get over being called dirty" (p. 25).

Losing the Data

There are a number of things that can happen to carefully collected data. Despite warnings to back up information, interview tapes are accidently erased or recorded over. Custodians throw away artwork made by participants. Databases disappear.

Researchers also lose data when participants withdraw, and ethical guidelines indicate they can withdraw at any time. But, are there limits? Many students have confronted this question days, sometimes even hours, before defending their thesis. Often this happens when participants suddenly realize the thesis will be a public document. During interviews, participants may reveal something they later regretted saying. In some cases, their identity could be known as they spoke frankly about circumstances or others. When participants withdraw from a qualitative study, researchers should not use the data collected from them. Chapters have to be rewritten as if the person never existed. Problems are compounded in art-based research. What happens if the participant who withdrew appears in someone else's photo? This practice differs in some quantitative and clinical studies, and students should consult their university's ethics office before using or destroying data.

Participants may be surprised to read their transcripts or find they disagree with how the researcher characterized them when a provisional report is given to them for verification. This is called member checking, and it allows participants to verify information and know how the data concerning them is interpreted. Sandelowski (1993) posits that participants may withdraw after reading the written excerpts pertaining to them because "the effect of seeing in print what they once said or listening to themselves on tape may be similar to seeing oneself on videotape giving birth: somewhat bizarre and not wholly comfortable" (p. 6). Sandelowski adds that, "Whereas members may strive to be accepted as good people, researchers typically strive to be accepted as good scholars: these goals may conflict" (p. 5). After reading their accounts, even if accurate, some participants may elect to withdraw from the study.

Students should anticipate this but not dispense with the member check as Sandelowski suggests. Participants have the right to read what is written about them and to determine if they want to be part of a study. Member checking is an on-going process conducted throughout the research process and should be initiated as early as possible. If participants elect to withdraw, they can either be replaced or not be part of the study and the student will not get the dreaded call from a participant the night before the oral defense.

Researchers should not attempt to convince participants to remain part of the study. Participants may find the research does not match their original conception. Or, they may have concerns of what will happen when the data they provide is made public. They may not trust that their identity will remain confidential. This is a possibility, because in small groups, complete anonymity is hard to achieve. According to Saunders, Kitzinger, and Kitzinger (2014), "Researchers must balance two competing priorities: maximizing protection of participant's identities and maintaining the value and integrity of the data" (p. 2). They advise that doing so requires an ongoing discussion between the researcher and participants, and this can be time consuming. On a practical note for students, member checking can be difficult because participants do not return their transcripts or sections written about them, and some do not give them much attention. Graduate students should take this into consideration when developing a timeline. It should also be determined who has the final authority over the interpretation. What if participants disagree with the researchers interpretation? Concerning group research, does one participant speak for all?

Faulty Data

Not all our data are to be trusted. This may be the case in survey research. For example, Robinson-Cimpian (2014) found that 19% of teens falsely claimed to be adopted, as seen in follow-up interviews with their parents, and in another study, 99% of 253 students falsely claimed to use an artificial limb. On the other hand, participants may give answers they believe the researcher wants or needs, wanting to please them or be helpful. Just as researchers are negotiating their sense of self as researchers, participants, too, are forming and maintaining a research identity. Teachers who conduct action research may find students behave differently because they consider themselves to be "guinea pigs." They may either want to please or be mischievous.

Conclusion

When conducting research, no one is immune to Murphy's Law: Whatever can go wrong, will. However, graduate research also is about what learning and failure can teach as much as success. Streiner and Sidani's (2010) book, *When Research Goes off the Rails: Why It Happens and What You Can Do About It* recounts the narratives of 42 researchers who tell readers that even when research does not go as planned, all is not lost. The chapters are instructive and hopeful in that they are drawn from successfully defended theses. We can vicariously learn from other's accounts of bumpy roads and running off the rails, but our own failures are most instructive.

Researchers cannot anticipate the complexity of the research process. There are safeguards they can take to prevent some data disasters. The first is to not be in a hurry to collect data. Pilot test all recording devises and be at ease with the technology. Pilot all questionnaires and interview questions. Use a validated survey or questionnaire. A DIY questionnaire may not yield the data you need or want, and it takes a long time to validate. Establish rapport with participants and take time to listen to their concerns.

Adopt the strategy of iterative data collection and analysis. Transcribe and code as you collect data. This may seem counter intuitive, and many students experience a momentum to collect all the data at once. However, this means they will pay later when they begin the analysis. They may find they either collected too much data or missed opportunities to collect important data.

DATA ANALYSIS

If data collection is the play of thesis research, data analysis is the work. This is especially true for qualitative researchers and it is common to feel a sense of panic when facing the many pages of notes, transcripts, and images they have collected. Drowning is a metaphor often used to describe the experience researchers feel when first confronted with this enormous amount of data. The notion of drowning in data is derived from John Naisbitt's mixed metaphor, "We are drowning in information, but starved for knowledge." The sensation of drowning is caused by information overload and an inability to make sense of it. At a loss for what to do, many students turn to their supervisors. In the words of Kvale (1996), they plead in a despairing voice, "Rescue me from my 1000 pages—I cannot find my way out of the labyrinth" (p. 277). Kvale advises researchers to have a plan for analysis before collecting any data, and if one has failed to do so, trying to code after the fact is futile. However, writing a thesis is a learning process and it is possible to adopt a coding system after data have been amassed. Coding 1000 pages of data begins not by coding a single line or image. It begins by organizing the data and selecting an appropriate existing coding method.

Data analysis is a "systematic search for meaning" (Leech & Onwuegbuzie, 2007, p. 558). Most texts and guidebooks refer to qualitative analysis as an art, rather than science. Students seldom witness the data analysis process. Few may be fortunate to be members of a team, where they will be apprenticed on how to code and reduce data. In the published articles, the authors tell readers that the data was collected according to a methodology, then coded as if by saying an incantation, a magical word – grounded theory, axel coding, abracadabra. The author then proceeds to his or her interpretation of the data. To a novice researcher, it is as if a rabbit has been pulled out of a magician's hat. But, data analysis it isn't magic. Word count limitations prevent authors from describing the details of their coding process, and they must assume that readers will be familiar with their coding terminology. This implies expert-to-expert communication. As readers, we trust these authors have paid due diligence to the data. Novice researchers must take at face value that something was done to produce the results, but cannot rework the steps.

Starting Points

Students should first determine what their data are and organize them. For interviews, this means creating verbatim transcripts. When dealing with transcripts, there are practical things to consider and the decisions rest on the constraints of time and money. Kvale (1996) rightly notes that an hour interview can generate 25 pages of written text. Transcribing is a time-consuming task, and it costs a good deal of money to have someone else do it. There are advantages and disadvantages to both options. Hiring someone to transcribe can mean getting the job done faster and being free to work on other parts of the thesis. This is an advantage if students are in a hurry or not adept at transcribing skills. A professional can complete the task in a fraction of time it takes the novice, but expect to pay either by the page or by the hour.

Most of my students who elect to transcribe their data report the advantages of doing so. A written transcript is a reduction of data that omits a great deal of detail. A transcript cannot fully capture the complexity of the oral transaction. It does not indicate in real time the long pause or the quick answer or distinguish between the tentative response and the emphatic one. Students who transcribe their interviews themselves can recall the events and the context of the interview, making note of those details. Ideally, analysis is an iterative process that starts during data collection. However, students may face time and financial constraints that require them to collect as much data as quickly as possible. Some research requires travel to collect data, and students may be able to afford to travel only once. They collect as much data possible, leaving no time to transcribe and code in the field. Transcribing is a way for the student to return to the field, so to speak.

For some students, transcribing is a tedious chore and something best done in one sitting. They may set aside a few weeks or months to accomplish the task. However, there are advantages to transcribing an interview and coding it before going to the next interview. This offers an opportunity for comparison.

Organizing photographs and visual documentation is best done either chronologically, by theme, or grouped according to the participant who made them. Backing up image files is important and students should dedicate a separate hard drive to keep these files.

Coding the Data

Qualitative research requires the researcher to interpret and make sense of the data. Description reports the data, while analysis is interpretation.

It tells what the data mean. Qualitative data analysis involves two phases: decontextualization and recontextualization (Starks & Trinidad, 2007). During decontextualization, the researcher separates the data from its original context and assigns codes. Saldaña (2013) explains, "A code in qualitative inquiry is most often a word or a short phrase that symbolically assigns a summative, salient, essence-capturing, and/or evocative attribute for a portion of language-based or visual data" (p. 3). Admittedly, many guidebook authors provide examples of how this is done but readers may be unable to draw the link between the excerpt and the code assigned to it. This is because as Saldaña posits, "Coding is not a precise science; it's primarily an interpretive act" (p. 4).

While it is true that data coding is an art, it is also a craft. Many students begin coding their data ad hoc. This usually involves going through transcripts and field notes, line-by-line, in a DIY fashion in hopes themes will emerge. This is a self-defeating method of analysis. Students do not need to invent a strategy. Saldaña offers 24 strategies for coding qualitative data. Similarly, Leech and Onwuegbuzie (2007) identified 21 methods but found most researchers conflate coding with grounded theory's constant comparison. Here, the researcher reads through the entire data set, such as a complete interview, and categorizes the data into meaningful parts by labeling each category with a code. The researcher then codes the next interview and compares the instances of the codes with the data previously labeled with the same code. Originally, this method was intended to analyze data collected over several iterations, but researchers have modified it to analyze data collected in one sitting (Charmaz, 2006).

Just as the goals and final products of the various qualitative methodologies differ, so do their conventions for coding data. For example, a classification system is best used to search for cultural knowledge, where as coding for a narrative analysis is holistic, viewing the narratives as a whole, rather than the sum of their parts. Charmaz (2006) provides a concise strategy for grounded theory coding, starting with word-by-word, line-by-line, and incident-to-incident coding. Following an existing coding strategy will help students to clearly articulate in the thesis the steps used to code and reduce the data. This is called an audit trail.

Some researchers consider intercoder reliability to be an important part of coding. Here, two or more researchers coding the same data should come to a close agreement on the codes. However, as qualitative research is interpretive, it is not likely two researchers will come to the same interpretation. The researcher should be able to explain his or her coding system to another and ask them to apply the code to data. The value in doing this is not to agree on the codes, but that explaining the coding strategy to others ensures researchers actually have a method. It is part of the audit trail of a decision-making process.

Coding visual images and film is considerably more complex than coding written texts. How images mean is as important as what they mean. Before asking what these forms mean, researchers must ask, "How do images create meaning?" Photographs and other forms of art are personal records and insights, constructed and framed by the artist. Images are more than their subject matter. For Sturken and Cartwright (2001) meaning is dependent on the social, political, and cultural context in which images are viewed. They are complex constructions and researchers who use images must learn their codes. There are number of strategies for interpreting images, but no universal method of analysis. Sturken and Cartwright, for example, employ a strategy of semiotics to coding and decoding images. Semiotics is the production of social meaning through a system of signs.

Barrett's (1990) book *Criticizing Photographs: An Introduction to Understanding Images* provides a framework to analyze and interpret photographs, and can be extended to other art forms. He distinguishes between internal and external sources of information. Internal information is that which the viewer sees when looking at the work: subject matter, its form, and style. External information includes the historical and social context in which it was taken and information about the photographer. Analysis takes both internal and external information into consideration. However, Barrett cautions researchers to not rely solely on the photographer's intent when making an interpretation. An artist can mean to express one thing, but viewers may interpret work in another way. For Barrett, viewers cannot fully know the artist's intent. Artworks can mean what the artist intended, but they can also mean much more.

Computer Assisted Qualitative Data Analysis Software (CAQDAS)

Given the labor intensity and subjective nature of coding data, many researchers have welcomed help from Computer Assisted Qualitative Data AnalysiS software (CAQDAS). These programs can help researchers organize and retrieve their data. Silver and Lewins (2015) provide a detailed discussion about technical support from improved and smaller mobile recording devises to software that can help researchers transcribe interviews. Although, to date, no software exists that can produce a transcript, voice recognition software packages allow a single researcher to dictate a text into a machine-readable format (Silver & Lewins, p. 606). This is useful for dictating field notes and can offer relief to those who have hand and wrist problems. Students who experience writer's block can explain their data verbally and later revise the draft. Some CAQDAS can combine data from mixed method research, combining and converting qualitative and quantitative data.

Leech and Onwuegbuzie (2007) caution researchers, "flexibility, creativity, insight, and intuition should never be replaced by a systematic and mechanical analysis of qualitative data" (p. 578). "Key to your understanding of the value of these packages are two words: assisted and tools. The software will not do any analysis for you, but it may serve as an able assistant and valuable tool" (p. 128). However, I imagine people expressed similar concerns when libraries began to use search engines rather than card catalogues. The biggest drawback of most software programs is the time they take to learn and use effectively. However, students who master one or more packages may find they are more efficient and have more time to devote to their research.

It is important to note that coding is not something that is done to the data once, and then the researcher moves on to interpret it. For, Saldaña it is a "cyclical act. Rarely is the first cycle of coding data perfectly attempted" (p. 8). Students should share excerpts of their coded data with others. This can be the supervisor or a critical friend. Ask "Have I overlooked anything? Is a bias evident? Have I focused only on data that agrees with my bias?" Getting early feedback can save valuable time. If a code term is wrong, the student will correct it before coding everything erroneously.

Interpreting the Data

Data are recontextualized through interpretation. Saldaña distinguishes between codes and themes, in that a theme is the outcome of coding. Themes allow researchers to make interpretations and connect their findings to themes found in the literature.

Trent and Cho (2015) borrow from Barrett's (2000) writing about art criticism to judge qualitative interpretations. I find Barrett's three criteria of coherence, correspondence, and inclusiveness to be most useful. Coherence asks, "Does it make sense?" Interpretations make sense when they tell a compete story. The interpretation should foremost make sense to the participants who provided the data. Correspondence asks, "Does the interpretation fit the data?" Students must make decisions on what to include and omit. Interpretation is speculative when the researcher draws conclusions without the data to support them. An interpretation is inclusive when it presents competing and contradicting points of view. Students should take care to avoid making statements that are not supported in the data or "cherry picking" the data that supports their arguments. Barrett (2000) points out that while there are no right or wrong interpretations, some interpretations are better than others. Students should strive for interpretations to be reasonable and convincing.

Ellis (2007) gives good advice for students who are writing about the lives of others. "I tell them to think about the ethical considerations before writing, but not to censure anything in the first draft to get the story as nuanced and truthful as possible" (p. 24). The drafts change and become nuanced with each iteration. I take Ellis's advice that students should share their interpretations with their participants, but not share their first drafts. When telling the research story, researchers must protect identities if they promised confidentiality. Saunders et al. (2014) claim this is a balancing act with competing priorities: "maximizing protection of participants' identities and maintaining the value and integrity of the data" (p. 2). They posit that anonymizing data is more than giving participants pseudonyms. It is also ensuring that potentially identifying information does not disclose the participant's identity to others. It may mean editing out specific identifying details.

CHAPTER 9

ESTABLISHING AN ACADEMIC TRACK RECORD

Not long ago, new graduates were hired on the basis of their promise. Today, they need proven track records that include conference presentations and peer-reviewed publications. They cannot wait for graduation to start building their Curriculum Vitae (CV), as competition for grants, post-doctorate positions, and jobs require that students are already active in their fields.

PRESENTING AT CONFERENCES

Giving a conference presentation can help relieve writer's block or get students out of the general malaise that comes from pouring over research for extended periods of time. Preparing for a public presentation can motivate students to write, construct charts, and verbally describe their data. Students can receive feedback from peers and established researchers who are working on the same topic. Attending presentations can make students aware of the trends and current research being conducted. Alternatively, attending a conference can devastate students' self-esteem and set their writing back months if their presentation does not go as well as planned. This section offers practical advice to ensure this will not happen.

Each discipline offers a number of conferences of different forms and sizes. They can range from large, annual national conferences hosted by associations, to small conferences built around a specific theme. Attendance can from range from thousands to fewer than one hundred people. Since attending conferences cost both time and money, students need to be strategic about presenting at a conference that is right for them.

It may be tempting to focus one's efforts on presenting at large, competitive association conferences, but if students are still collecting data or are in the early stages of analysis, it is advisable to wait. There are more appropriate venues to present research in progress and working papers. Graduate symposia do not have the status of a professional conference, but they can provide excellent opportunities. They are good places to practice public speaking and discuss early research results. It may be less costly to attend because they generally do not ask registration fees, and food and drinks may be provided. Graduate symposia can provide opportunities to network with one's peers and some are held at prestigious universities boasting highly respected faculty members. Many feature an established researcher as the keynote speaker. However, I agree with Mumby (2012) who recommends limiting the number of symposia. They are low risk, but offer low rewards. These conferences do not carry much weight on a CV. Students will only hear other graduate students presentations and will not learn from more experienced presenters.

Some smaller conferences may be less intimidating and can be more rewarding to attend. Novice presenters might have more people attend their presentations than they would at a large conference because they are not in competition with several concurrent sessions. Smaller events may also include time allotted for group dinners and for socializing. This may allow students to get to know established researchers better and may later help them suggest external examiners for their thesis.

Some conferences publish their proceedings, but these publications do not substitute for a peer-reviewed paper. Do not present a paper that has already been published or one that has been given at another conference. The correct order of events is to present a paper, hear feedback and respond, and then submit for publication. A paper with the same title and content presented at multiple conferences is only one CV entry. Moreover, the same people may attend the same conferences and they will not want to hear the same paper twice.

Before Submitting a Proposal

Conference organizers issue their call for papers well in advance of the conference. Calls for papers (CFP) are usually announced in association newsletters and on social media sites. Before responding to a call, there are some very important matters to consider. Those whose research is collaborative should make others aware of their intention to present research before submitting the proposal. I interviewed a professor who recounted a story about a student who had submitted an abstract to a prestigious conference without her knowledge. Although the professor did not regard the research as ready for dissemination, the paper was accepted. She was furious and contacted the organizers to withdraw the paper. Additionally, if you are planning a group presentation, determine who will present and the order of authorship. Some supervisors claim first author on research presentations that come from their labs and grants. Many conferences list only the first author in their catalogues.

Second, but of equal importance, calculate what it will cost to attend. Some conferences can cost hundreds of dollars for membership and registration. The registration fee is usually not mentioned in the call for papers. It may be possible to locate this information on the previous year's conference website. Additionally, inquire as to whether or not membership is required at the time of submission. Some professional organizations require a membership, but being a member is no guarantee of acceptance. Students usually are offered discounted membership fees and sometimes reduced registration fees.

Take into consideration any costs involved with travel and accommodations. Many conferences are held in large cities where hotels are expensive. Conference organizers reserve blocks of rooms at sponsored hotels and give discounts to their attendees. Sometimes, they must purchase the rooms and resell to those attending. If fewer than expected attend, the organization is required to pay for the unsold rooms so they block fewer than the expected attendance. Those who regularly attend annual conferences book rooms immediately after the venue is announced, even before they have a confirmation of acceptance. This ensures they will get the room at the conference discount. There may be less expensive hotels nearby, but those may fill early. It may be possible to secure a room and cancel if the proposal is not accepted. If travel requires a flight, consider travel costs to and from airports. Some cities do not offer public transportation and airports may be located away from the city center requiring costly taxi rides to and from the conference.

One expense that is frequently overlooked is going out for dinner and drinks. If you are invited to join your supervisor and another established researcher, this will cost. They can afford the restaurants. Eating out with peers is less costly, but this can still add up.

Determine who will be responsible to cover the conference costs. Supervisors may pay some or all, but do not expect the supervisor to pay for a conference in Fuji. Some universities offer travel bursaries to offset conference costs of presenting, but they usually cover a portion. Generally, they will pay registration and part of the travel expenses. Also, they will only pay if you have a paper accepted, not for attendance. Universities may require students to pay for the conference, and then submit receipts and proof of attendance and participation. It may take considerable time to be reimbursed.

How to Write a Conference Proposal

Typically, a conference proposal includes a title, a catalogue description, and a longer abstract (250 words). Some require completed papers, but that is the exception. Some conferences also ask for a brief CV or biography for each presenter.

Determine the preferred format of the presentation. There are a number of presentation formats, which include keynote addresses, super-sessions, single papers, panels, poster sessions, as well as alternative forms, such as the Pecha Kucha, and the 3-minute elevator speech. Well-known researchers and authors who are usually paid make keynote addresses. They are featured prominently with a photo and bio in the conference procedures. Next is the hour-long, single authored presentation. Shorter papers, usually 25 minutes, may be grouped together in 60 or 90 minute sessions. Panels, which are predetermined when submitting a proposal, can include a number of presenters, each who will speak for a few minutes. In order to be financially viable, conferences need people to attend, and most attend only if they make a presentation. Organizers maximize room usage with new formats. Many conferences feature poster sessions where only the amount of space determines how many can participate. Resembling a science fair from elementary school, researchers create a poster to illustrate their findings and stand by it hoping people will walk by to inquire about their research. Some conferences give prizes, which encourage participation.

Graduate students should not attempt an hour, single authored paper until they have several presentations under their belt. Those who are not comfortable speaking publically might consider presenting as part of a panel. This will mean less pressure and increases the likelihood more people will attend. However, it is not uncommon to request a paper session, but be offered another format such as a poster session.

The presentation title is vitally important. It will outlive the presentation and as a CV entry, it will follow you for your academic career. The title should be informative and engaging. Avoid inside jokes, irony, and anything sexually suggestive or vulgar. It should be descriptive of your presentation. Do not repeat the title in the catalogue description. Words are precious, so do not waste them by writing, "In this presentation, I will attempt to..." Tell what you will do and how your research connects to conference theme and to the audience.

Pay careful attention to the conference theme. A major reason why presentations are rejected is because the author ignored the theme (Haas, 2014). When writing the proposal, make a clear connection to the theme and consider who will be in the audience. Ask yourself, why should the audience care about your presentation? Appeal to a wide audience but avoid promising more than can be delivered. Have the data been analyzed? Before submitting a hopeful abstract, consider if the paper will actually be written. While it may be common to see professors writing their papers on the plane, students cannot take such risks. Data collection can go wrong or the analysis may not be as advanced as originally thought.

Adhere to the specified word count and submission deadlines. It is unlikely you will be given an extension or a later deadline. Some conferences organizers extend their deadlines, but that usually means they did not get enough submissions.

Submit a proposal only when there is a reasonable chance of attendance. Having a paper accepted to a conference and then not attending is deplorable. Some conference organizers keep data bases of no-shows. Do not under any circumstance simply not show. If something presents you from attending, alert the organizers well in advance before they book rooms and print the program. One group posted their program online and anyone who cancelled got a big red "cancelled" sign over his or her presentation.

How to Make a Conference Presentation

Before preparing the paper and visuals, review the abstract and proposal. Ensure you are presenting what the abstract promised. There are usually numerous simultaneous presentations and the members of the audience chose this presentation over the others based on the catalogue description. If the presenter does not deliver, they will walk out, slamming the door behind them.

Presenters owe their audience the courtesy of being prepared. Never apologize for not being prepared. Be prepared. The best way to ensure a presentation will go well is to practice it in front of others. If this isn't possible, practice it alone, but aloud. Know your material and the order of the presentation. Presenting at a conference is not the same as presenting to a class. Presenting, whether in a group or alone, is a skill. Engage with the audience.

When presenting with a panel, or as a paper within a group of other papers, it is essential to stay within the time limit. The extra time one presenter takes comes directly from someone else's time, and those who do not respect the rules are not asked to be on future panels. It is a wonderful to be asked a question at the end of the presentation, but do not monopolize the conversation. Answer the questions briefly and perhaps direct a question toward other members of the panel.

Have excellent visuals, but do not rely on technology to do the speaking. PowerPoint, Prezi, or the latest way of showing data is a tool, not the presenter.

Know the material and deliver it enthusiastically. A common mistake presenters make is putting too much text on a slide. It can't be read and it upstages the presenter. Another problem is relying solely on technology. No power, no point. Printed handouts can save a presentation if something goes wrong.

Preparing posters require time and highly developed graphic design skill. Purrington (2014) offers free templates online, suggests software, and provides a lengthy list of dos and don'ts. An added bonus of this useful site is his dry sense of humor.

It is impossible to estimate the number of people who will be in your audience. Do not take it personally if you have few in attendance and be very cordial to those who do attend. You may be competing with 35 other presentations, or been slated during a keynote address or a business meeting of the association. Conferences can run for several days and there are peak times to present. Conference organizers seem to employ a hierarchy that tacitly indicates your station in the academic world. Presenters deemed important are given more time to present than those deemed less important. Usually the first full day of the conference and between 10am and 2pm is considered optimum. Prior to that, people are arriving, getting set up, and later, conference fatigue sets in. Students are often given the early morning, evening, or last day slots. However, regardless of the presentation time or form, all are peer-reviewed and attendance is not noted on CVs. It makes no difference if it is standing room only or if only one person attends. Even if only one person attends your presentation, perform as if that person is the most important person at the conference. Give a presentation worthy of a keynote address.

How to Attend Presentations and Network

Some people go to conferences to present, and then ignore anything else. This is not what students should do. Attend sessions by peers as well as by well-known researchers. Your peers may become the established researchers of tomorrow. These are your valuable colleagues. You will review each other's work and collaborate on future research. Many conferences offer sessions on how to write for academic journals, usually given by editors and members of the review board. They offer inside information and valuable publishing tips.

Conferences can be places where academics behave badly, but doing so will not serve you well. When attending presentations, avoid trying to score points by pointing out other's obvious mistakes. If someone makes an error, address it in private. Ask questions to elaborate or discuss, not to show the flaw in the presentation. Academics have excellent memories and the person being attacked may well be a member of your hiring committee.

Writing about conferences for historians, Iacovetta and Taylor-Ladd (2010) posit, "As a novice, you're supposed to make yourself known to established scholars in your field, but no one knows quite how to do it" (p. 50). Indeed, this is a challenge. Academics run in packs and many of the established researchers hang out with other established researchers. They may be planning their next grant or book, or simply catching up, and you are not invited to be part of the conversation. Even if you do get a brief moment with them, they probably won't remember your name no matter how clever your elevator speech was. Iacovetta and Taylor-Ladd aptly remind students to not take this personally, that most are "also seeing friends and colleagues whose company they rarely get a chance to enjoy" (p. 50).

It is difficult to network on one's own. Supervisors may introduce students to other researchers and even them invite to dinner. Students cannot crash the party, and if their supervisor is a conference recluse, they are on their own. A better strategy is to identify a couple established researchers that you would like to meet. Why do you want to meet them? What questions might you have about their work? Read their work and prepare a thoughtful question before hand. Attend their presentations and write to them after they return to their universities.

HOW TO PUBLISH A JOURNAL ARTICLE

Increasingly, in addition to presenting at conferences, students are expected to publish papers before obtaining their degrees. Thesis examiners and future employers look favorably on student publications, but most students have little understanding of how to publish a paper or of publishing culture. This section describes the peer-review process and offers suggestions to get papers published. It also considers intellectual property rights and conceptions of authorship.

Selecting the Appropriate Journal

Every researcher's goal is to publish her or his findings in a prestigious journal, but starting with the most prestigious journal in the field and working down the list in hopes one will accept the paper is not the best strategy for publishing. This is a time consuming process and authors are likely to hit bottom with the same flawed paper with which they started. Pilot projects, literature reviews, works in progress, commentaries, and revised course papers are rarely published in top-tier journals. Moreover, these papers may be subjected to cruel reviews, which can shake a novice author's confidence. The most effective way to approach publishing is to start with a journal that best fits your topic and stage of research. Although this may mean the targeted journal has less academic impact, it may allow for an easier time getting the paper into the public domain.

Supervisors likely have good knowledge of the journals in their field and can suggest the best venue for your research. Before writing, become familiar with the journal. Locate and read the writer's contribution page, or manuscript submission guidelines, paying close attention to word counts and page limits. Read several papers recently published in the journal, noting their format, tone, and methodology. Most academic journals adhere to similar conventions, which mirror the proposal and thesis. Papers begin with a clear statement of purpose, followed by a literature review, a methodology section, and analysis and discussion.

Journals often hold specific theoretical stances and values about the field. Do not select a journal and attempt to write in opposition. It is highly unlikely the *Journal of Teaching Social Justice* will publish a paper titled "Why teaching about social justice is wrongheaded." Similarly, if a journal publishes quantitative research, the reviewers will not accept a paper from data drawn from a qualitative study. If available, read the editorial page, which often indicates the kinds of research the editor would like to publish. Many editors present sessions about writing for their journals at conferences where they offer style tips and suggestions about upcoming issues.

Understanding the Peer-Review Process

Often, editors select reviewers, who serve for a three to five year term. Editors also serve for a specific length of time and some reviewers' service overlaps with two editors. Reviewers are the peers in the peer-review process. Blind review means reviewers receive papers with no author names. They are usually assigned these papers because their interest and expertise matches that of the author. In small fields with niche journals, reviewers can often guess the identity of the author with a fair amount of accuracy.

Reviewers are tasked with reading a submission and deciding on its fate. They can "accept," "accept with minor modifications," "accept with major modifications," or "reject." Journals differ in their resubmission policies in that some allow for unlimited resubmissions, provided the paper is seen to be inching toward acceptance. Others allow for a limited number of resubmissions, after which the paper is rejected. Reviewers rarely accept a paper "as written." Authors are usually given recommendations for improving the manuscript. Papers accepted with minor revisions are left to the discretion of the editor. Papers judged to need "major modifications" are returned to the original reviewer for judgment, provided that person's term is not over. If his or her term has expired, the paper will be sent to another reviewer, who may or may not agree with the first reviewer. In some cases, the editor may "desk reject" the papers he or she deems to be of poor quality or not fitting the journals objectives (SAGE, n.d). Desk rejected papers are not sent to reviewers.

Reviewers are also asked to provide written comments. Some are kind and start with positive comments, followed by suggestions for improvement. Some treat the review process as a blood sport and (appear) to relish destroying egos. Some reviewers promptly return reviewed papers, while others do not. Serving as a reviewer is voluntary and is considered to be service to the field. Editors and managing editors can send reminders, but they depend on the good will of a reviewer to return a paper by the specified deadline.

Board directors from organizations sponsoring the journal usually have the task of selecting editors for the journal. They frequently pull from those who have published in the journal and are active researchers. The position of editor is prestigious and powerful. According to Donovan (2007), editor of a number of journals, editors "wield considerable power and it is not too much to say that an editorial decision made during a critical review period may make or break a career" (p. 152). Editors know their reviewers, and know which reviewers are sympathetic and give would-be authors a chance to revise. They also know those who outright reject papers. If two reviewers disagree, the editor makes the final call on the status of the paper. Then, the editor decides which accepted papers appear in the journal. Some editors accept more papers than they publish and accepted papers may languish for years in the archives. These "in press" papers have no impact, which is measured by the number of times other researchers cite them.

Some journals make special calls for papers on a specific topic. If accepted, the paper will likely be published in a faster time. However, deadlines and revisions times are shorter, if permitted at all. Even if the paper is accepted with major modifications, it is not likely to be included in the journal because there is no time to revise and resubmit.

What Is an Author?

Some students have been surprised to discover their names had been omitted from publications to which they believed they contributed. Perhaps they conducted a literature review, or collected and coded data. This section explores the questions about student authorship and examines student contribution to published papers. Student intellectual property rights raise a number of questions. Is the student the sole author of papers emerging from the thesis? Are research assistants entitled to authorship?

Most universities have authorship policies specific to student research, but there is no universal agreement on who has the right to be an author of a paper. Some universities have adopted and modified guidelines from organizations such as the Committee on Publication Ethics (COPE) (2014) or the APA Science Student Council (2006). COPE, for example, recommends that authors meet four criteria: a substantial contribution to the conception or design or process of the research, drafting the work for publication, making the final approval of the version to be published, and being accountable for all aspects of the work, including its accuracy and integrity. The University of Toronto School of Graduate Studies (2007), for example, requires authors to contribute to two of four criteria: conception or design of the research, data collection, analysis, and writing the manuscript. In this instance, students who collect data only would not be considered authors.

Controversial and unethical authorship practices exist and are discouraged by journal editors and policy makers. These include guest, gift, and ghost authors. A guest author is a high profile researcher whose name has been added to a submission in hopes it will raise the paper's profile and improve its chances for publication. The authors believe the editor will be more generous with the paper and the guest's name ensures it will get into print faster. Guests make no contribution to the paper. Similarly, gift authors make little or no contribution, and their names appear as a gift. In some departments, the department chair is given or expects the gift of co-authoring papers from his or her colleagues. Perhaps this practice originated to thank those willing to take on administrative positions that provide service at the expense of their own research productivity. However, known cases of abuse of power have caused many journal editors to eschew this practice. Assistant professors may be coerced to include senior faculty members on their papers in fear they will not receive tenure. Some students are required to "gift" papers emerging from their thesis to their supervisors.

Ghosts authors are paid to write papers for which the listed authors take full credit. The name and contribution of the ghost are not acknowledged.

When discovered, this practice can damage a university and researcher's reputation. This has been witnessed in medical research where pharmaceutical companies provide publishable papers for the researchers who are testing their drugs. For students, hiring a ghost author to write a paper or part of the thesis is considered academic misconduct.

To curb guest, gift, and ghost authorship practices, some journal editors ask that each author be able to describe his or her contribution to the paper. All authors should make substantial contributions to research, data analysis, and drafting of the manuscripts on which their name appears.

A number of people may contribute to a paper or a body of research but do not meet the criteria of author. They may be responsible for acquiring research funding, supervising a research group, or providing general administrative support. Other contributors provide writing assistance, technical editing, language editing, and proofreading. These individuals should be thanked in the acknowledgement of the paper but should not be listed as authors.

The Order of Authors

Frequently, papers are the result of research conducted by teams or groups of individuals. The order of authorship signals to readers, who are in the know, which person made the greatest contribution to the paper. This is an example of tacit knowledge, and rarely do course instructors think to impart this knowledge when discussing papers. Authorship and the order the names appear on a published paper are important if students intend to use the papers as part of their thesis. Students in this case need to demonstrate that their contribution was substantial.

Authorship conventions are discipline specific. In the humanities and social sciences, the first author is the person who has made the most contribution to the paper. Additional authors line up like planets in the solar system, with the last being the furthest from the sun. In disciplines in the sciences and engineering, the last author signifies the person who provides funding for the research and supervises the lab. In this case, the last author is responsible to ensure all data presented in the paper is correct. Still others, such as math and physics, use alphabetic order to indicate equal contribution.

When considering the order of authors of a co-authored paper, it is important to negotiate and make clear the roles before writing the paper, and to revisit the decision throughout the writing process. Disputes arise when research teams fail to do this and disputes after the fact are difficult to resolve to everyone's satisfaction. The APA Science Student Council (2006) provides a research responsibility checklist that identifies the various tasks associated with publishing research, such as obtaining ethics approval, writing the report, and contacting participants. The form guides the decision making process and allows students and faculty to consider all the tasks a published paper requires. The form helps students understand their role and be aware of the expected time commitment before agreeing to work on a paper. Everyone should understand what is expected of authors and contributors to avoid unpleasant surprises when the paper appears in print.

Before writing a paper, all members of the research team should anticipate and solve all concerns. Begin by identifying and weighing all the tasks required to write the paper. From this, determine who will be the lead author and who will contribute to writing the paper. A peer who knows he or she is fifth author will do the work of such, and not invest the time expected of a first author. However, roles can change throughout the writing process and some people can overestimate the significance of their contribution.

Authorship of papers from students' theses is an area of contention. Many students, rightly, believe the theses to be their intellectual property. They collected and analyzed the data, and wrote the final manuscript. Supervisors, on the other hand, believe their contribution in shaping their students' research, and reading and responding to multiple drafts entitles them to co-authorship. Some provided funding and lab space, and the ideas that guided the research. Generally, students in the humanities and social sciences are the sole authors of their thesis research, but practices differ among universities and programs.

Students should inquire if their university, department, or research team has a policy on authorship and intellectual policy before committing to work on a publication. In some cases, supervisors automatically assume first author on publications that result from research conducted in their labs or when they are the primary investigator (PI) of a funded research project. When working collaboratively and as part of a supervisor's research grant, it is important to discuss issues of intellectual property. Who owns and is entitled to publish the data from research? For example, University of Toronto students do not own intellectual property collected as a result of employment (University of Toronto, 2007). In other words, data collected by students hired as research assistants belong to the employer. Data collected by and for the student belong to the student.

Admittedly, knowing one's rights and having the power to exercise them are two different things. In truth, students have very little power over authorship and order of authors. This power sits squarely with their supervisors, and most students are not in a position to negotiate. It is possible that supervisors who take credit for their student's work are re-enacting the same abuses of power to which they were subjected as students, continuing a vicious cycle. If gift and ghosting are departmental or program practices, there is little one student can do to change the system. However, it is my hope that students reading this book will not perpetuate a broken system and will instill a culture of fairness and honesty when they become supervisors.

Some journals have policies that prohibit authors from publishing the same data more than once and the supervisor should determine when and how to disseminate data collected as a group. Students planning to write or present about data collected as part of their supervisors' research should discuss this with their supervisors before doing so. Supervisors are responsible for protecting the reputation of their labs and the rights of other students. When submitting a paper written for a course, the instructor should be notified of the intention to publish as a courtesy. A paper written for a class is most likely to be the intellectual property of the student and the instructor's contribution should be acknowledged in the paper. Often the instructor is an expert on the subject and has carefully selected course reading that shape the question. Good instructors read carefully and give feedback. They often encourage students to publish the paper and even suggest possible journals. However, most course papers require substantial revisions to meet publication standards.

How to Submit a Paper

Before submitting the paper, proofread it for any spelling mistakes. Read it forwards and backwards. Read it out loud. Numerous minor errors put reviewers in a bad mood and they may no longer trust you. Check the references for accuracy and format. Ask two peers to read the paper. Silva (2007) recommends that papers should be submitted "as perfect as possible" and "only masochists submit rough drafts to journals" (p. 90). Reviewers are not copy editors or coauthors, and as such resent being asked to correct papers. If they encounter errors early in the paper, they will not continue reading to find its merits.

A cover letter to the editor should accompany any paper sent to the journal. The cover letter informs the editor that the paper has not been submitted for consideration elsewhere. In other words, authors cannot submit the same paper to several journals at the same time in hopes one will accept it. Doing so is unethical and can damage an author's career. Submitting a previously published paper to another journal is self-plagiarism, and if detected by the editor or reviewers, will cause the paper to be rejected. The cover letter should also provide assurances the research received ethical approval, and permission was obtained to use any copyrighted materials appearing in the paper.

Many journals have long turnaround times. These depend on the schedules of the reviewers including their on grant deadlines, end of semester grading, and summer holidays.

How to Deal with Reviewers' Comments

At times, most authors will receive reviews with which they disagree or that imply the author is a first year undergraduate student. Accept criticism as part of the learning process and do not take it personally. It is possible that the author has inadvertently written something that deeply offends the reviewer. It is also possible that the reviewer is having a bad day. The author can never know which is the case.

Once the reviews are received, read them and then put them side. Talk to friends. Read them again on another day. Resist all urges to write to the editor. Instead, revise according to the reviews and resubmit within two to three weeks. The faster authors make the revisions, the more likely the paper will be returned to the same reviewer.

When resubmitting, write a detailed cover letter to the editor addressing how each revision was addressed. Do not ignore the reviews. Usually, reviewers ask for more details and examples. This means authors must add to the paper, which is already at the word limit. Before exceeding the limit, contact the editor for a grace of a few words. Be prepared to cut from other sections rather than add more pages. Editors know the limits for publication and are reluctant to extend them.

Why Papers Are Rejected

Papers are likely to be rejected when they do not fit the journal and when authors demonstrate no concern for the journal's readership. Other reasons may include ignoring page limits. It is possible the paper was hastily written and submitted before authors took time to revise and proofread. Donovan (2007) adds that journals hold "geographical prejudices" (p. 154) and publish papers concerned with North America or Europe. While that may or may not be true, all authors must take their readers in mind, and ask, why would someone read this? What does it matter? Papers should address recent literature and support the author's claims. Many rejected papers are speculative commentary rather than reports of solid research.

Rejection is part of publishing and reviewer's comments help improve a paper. Donovan recommends revising and submitting to another journal but warns, "A bad, rejected paper, submitted elsewhere and without any improvement, is still bad and is always likely to be returned" (p. 154). However, authors can take comfort in Silva's (2007) words, "A good paper will always find a home" (p. 107).

FINDING SUPPORT FOR WRITING THE THESIS

INTRODUCTION

By the time graduate students begin to write the thesis, which involves crafting a cohesive story from all the research components, many have written numerous course papers and some have even published in peer-reviewed journals. They have written and defended a thesis proposal and some have passed extensive comprehensive exams. Why, then, do so many students fail to finish their programs? Virginia Wolfe famously wrote, "A woman must have money and a room of her own if she is to write fiction." This chapter takes up the question, "What does a graduate student need to write a thesis?" In addition to Wolfe notions of money and a space to write, graduate students need time, motivation, and supervisor support. This chapter offers strategies that help students make the most of their time and secure support and motivation from their supervisors.

Time

Anne, a recent graduate, had worked on her thesis for a number of years and was near the time limit allowed by her university. Last summer, she focused all her energies on finishing her thesis. One day, her young daughter came to her, asking her to play. Anne explained that she was working and would play with her later. Her daughter looked at her and asked, "Mommy, when will you be fun again?"

Anne's story echoes that of many graduate students who must choose between academia and their life, which must be placed on hold in order to finish the thesis. Byers et al (2014) examined the survival strategies of ten doctoral students and found, "They often felt guilt (i.e., feelings that their studies were taking time away that could be spent with family or friends) and worry (i.e., concern they might not be able to meet the challenges of the program)" (p. 123). Putting aside the thesis to take a walk in the forest, to have dinner with friends, or to take children to the park brings unbelievable joy. These fleeting positive moments are soon replaced by guilt and worry.

Students who were both lucky and unlucky to obtain faculty positions while ABD (all but dissertation) find the stress to be magnified. Many take offers before completing because they need the money and fear another offer will not come along. This is the proverbial offer you can't refuse. Students who take tenure track positions and try to write their thesis find themselves in a double bind of attending to competing goals. They must publish and present to ensure tenure, and finish their thesis as a student. Similarly, students may need to work, some taking on one or more jobs, which diminishes motivation to write considerably.

An abundance of self-help books on how to write a thesis line library bookshelves. Graduate students are the ideal audience for this literary genre. I surveyed a number of books available from my library and found most offered some valuable advice. Like diet books, they will yield positive results, provided readers follow the advice offered. I note, however, that most of books were still on the shelf leading me to believe they are not being used. While there is a great deal of research and advice being dispensed about and to graduate students, most do not have the time to locate the information when they need it. A colleague remarked to me that when he was preparing to write his thesis, his supervisor gave him a copy of Joan Bolker's (1998) famed *Writing Your Thesis in Fifteen Minutes a Day: A Guide to Starting, Revising, and Finishing your Doctoral Thesis.*

"Did it help?" I asked.

"I didn't have time to read it. I had to write my dissertation" he replied.

The most useful advice provided by self-help books, such as those by Bolker (1998) and Silva (2007), is that to be productive, students must set aside time to write. Time is finite and everyone has demands competing for their attention. Silva, in *How to Write a Lot: A Practical Guide to Productive Academic Writing* recommends that writing needs to be a daily habit by making a schedule and adhering to it. Students who devote a full day once per week will accomplish less than those who work consistently an hour a day, every day. Students lose momentum after a couple of days. Working consistently keeps the thesis always on the mind. When the thesis is out of sight, it is out of mind. Time is spent trying to get back to the place they left off in the last writing session. In some cases, this involves remembering and locating the resources that have been filed away.

Bolker and Silva suggest writers treat their writing schedule as they would an important appointment with a doctor. Unlike teaching a class or other appointments, writing time is flexible. No one cares if you skip a day of writing, but everyone is concerned if you miss an appointment. Importantly, they also stress that writing requires persistence and it is a waste of time to attempt writing the perfect first draft. It is easier to revise a poorly written text than craft a brilliant one. For Silva, "The cure for writer's block—if you can cure a specious affliction—is writing" (p. 46).

Writing Support

Most supervisors do not know how to help students write, despite Paré's (2011) assertion that, "In a very real sense, doctoral supervisors are writing teachers" (p. 59). Most supervisors are researchers and teachers of discipline knowledge and are not trained to teach writing skills. Delamont, Parry, and Atkinson (1998) interviewed nearly 100 supervisors and found that many struggled to find the balance between "intervention and non-intervention in the student's writing" (p. 163). This involved deciding to either leave students to work through their writing problems on their own or "spoonfeeding" them (p. 160).

We learn language *in situ* and use it without reflection. McAlpine and Amundsen (2011) explain that academic language, like learning one's mother tongue, is a gradual process and rarely theorized. Perhaps supervisors believe that students will acquire this language and writing culture by reading published papers and mimicking them. Kiley (2009) suggests supervisors also know when a student is faking it as evidenced in this quote from an experienced supervisor, "My supervisor used to say fake it until you make it" (p. 296). While a certain amount of mimicry is necessary, it is not a substitute for mastery.

Students can find help from style guides specific to their discipline. A thesis in biology will have a different tone, style and format than will one in Art History. Academic culture is embedded in language and form. For example, in my field, we tend to write theses as narratives, which explain and describe. We do not formulate arguments. When a student writes, "I will argue that…" we are taken aback. Students need to know if they should write in first person or in third. Does the discipline use passive voice or active voice? How do researchers position themselves in the research?

Many students use books about methodology to write their proposals, but stop at the data analysis chapter. These books hold valuable information on how to write in that specific methodology. For example, it is a mistake for those conducting action research and PAR to refer to themselves as "the researcher." Herr and Anderson (2015) explain, "This typically is a sign that the action researcher (or his or her dissertation committee) lacks a fundamental understanding of the epistemology of the insider action research" (p. 43).

Motivation

Spaulding and Rockinson-Szapkiw (2012) point out that motivation is a key factor in persistence to complete a degree, and working with a supportive supervisor is essential to motivation. Motivation from supervisors comes is many forms and it cannot be understated how important it is to receive feedback from a supervisor when writing the thesis. It is important to get feedback early in the writing stage and there are some ways to accomplish this. Graduate students often initiate the feedback cycle by sending the supervisor a draft. Frequently, they complain that they do not receive feedback or that supervisors are ignoring them. Many wonder if they should send reminders, and question how long they should wait for a response. The problem is twofold: the work was unsolicited and it is not the supervisor's first priority to respond. Students should not send work in progress, without warning, with the request, "Can you take a look at this and tell me if I am going in the right direction?" Before sending work to a supervisor, the student needs to meet with their supervisor.

How to Meet with a Supervisor

Working with a supervisor is a professional, not a social, exchange. It does not mean students shouldn't like their supervisor or socialize with them. It means that this is an academic relationship and to get the best advice and mentorship from a supervisor, the student should treat the supervisor's time as one would any other busy professional. This section tells how to make the most of those meetings.

Be on time and never miss an appointment. Frequently, students email or call to tell their supervisor they will be "a few minutes late." Although the reasons may be quite legitimate and unavoidable, the time missed will come out of the time set to discuss the thesis research. Being late means that a meeting scheduled for an hour is now 45 minutes, or less. If, on the other hand, the supervisor is late, wait at least 20 minutes. Although this is no excuse, committee meetings can run overtime. However, the meeting with the student should not be rushed to make up for lost time.

If the supervisor does not show up for the meeting, take note of the day and time of the scheduled meeting. Follow up with an email inquiring if you had made a mistake and scheduled the wrong time or day. Mistakes can happen, but the purpose of this email is to establish communication and to keep a record of missed meetings. The following chapter deals with unavailable or unresponsive supervisors and keeping a record will help in dealing with that kind of a situation.

At times, students need to meet their supervisor to obtain signatures on various forms. In these cases, ensure that the form is completed as much as possible before the meeting. The focus of the meeting is to keep the thesis moving forward and nothing should distract that goal.

Come to the meeting with a tentative agenda and specific questions pertaining to the research. Take careful notes of the discussion during the meeting. Supervisors dislike receiving a follow up email asking them to repeat the information and sources they provided during the meeting. They may ignore these emails or repeat one or two sources, grudgingly. Or they may forget what was suggested. However, it is acceptable and recommended to follow up with questions if the information given was not clear.

At the end of the meeting, determine what work will be completed for the next meeting, and agree on the date it will be sent to the supervisor. Supervisors who receive a lengthy rough draft hours before a meeting should not be expected to comment on it during the meeting. In the beginning of the writing process, it is a good idea to take on smaller pieces of research for feedback. At first, students underestimate the amount of time needed to write, and it is better to commit to producing small amounts rather than to be overly ambitious and fail. Together, confirm a date for the next meeting. This should be a mutually agreed upon amount of time, but it should be, at a minimum, once per month. Take care to not get into a vicious cycle where students, believing they are not producing fast enough, avoid meeting with their supervisor. This is a mistake on the part of the student. Regularly scheduled meetings are key to keep students motivated.

No later than the day after the meeting, send an email, which includes a short memo of the important points discussed. This email should be carefully written and free of typos and grammatical errors. Here, the student can ask for clarity if, for example, a recommendation was confusing. This email should confirm the date of the next meeting and reiterate when the promised work will be sent to the supervisor. This email establishes a track record of meetings, and reminds you of your homework. It also provides a record of the supervisor's availability. Should the supervisor's unavailability cause delays that cost the student time and money, these email exchanges will support the case to change supervisors. Students with co-supervisors should copy all correspondence to both supervisors to ensure both are aware of the direction of the research and avoid inconsistent advice.

Setting clear deadlines for completing work eliminates the guesswork of when the student can expect feedback. Supervisors know when they can expect work and when they will meet to discuss it. If the supervisor knows when she or he will receive a hundred midterm exams, or an important grant is due, she or he can communicate that to the student. The student is not left in the dark as to when they will receive feedback. Some supervisors are relaxed and prefer meetings as needed, but I believe most will conform to the structure established by the student. If a supervisor is not willing to meet with students on a regular basis, then they need to consider if this is the right supervisor for them.

Once the deadline for work has been agreed upon, make it a priority to send the work in on time. Do not email to beg for extensions. If some event prevented the work from being completed, cancel the appointment and attempt to set new deadlines and meeting times. When sending the work, or in any correspondence, include the last email to remind the supervisor of what took place at the last the meeting. This serves as an *aide memoire* to help the supervisor place your work in a context. Popular supervisors may be working with several students and cannot recall the details of your research.

How to Ensure Good Feedback

Do not ask supervisors to read a rambling train of thought, run on sentences, or badly written first attempts. Submit a draft to the supervisor only after it is polished. First drafts are always tentative and no one except the writer should read them. The writer is establishing the tone and finding his or her voice. Self-doubt is part of the process, and knowing that no one will read what is written prevents writer's block. Always proofread and rework the text. Supervisors want to deal with big questions. They do not want to copyedit and many resent having to do so.

Before asking for the supervisor's help, return to the proposal and ask if what is written is in line with it. Does it address the research questions? If confirmation on the direction is still needed, provide the supervisor with a memo in outline or point form. Do not ask the supervisor to search for the meaning in pages of text. It is important that the student be clear about nature of the feedback needed. Ask specific questions about what to include, what to omit. "Is this OK?" will not yield informative answers. A vague question may receive an equally vague response. In most cases when supervisors give vague advice, they are not being negligent. Supervisors intuitively know when something is not working, but they are unable to articulate the problem.

They resort to phrases such as "you need to strengthen your argument," "more justification is needed," and "unpack this concept."

Communication breaks down when students are confused about what they think their supervisors want, or when supervisors believe they have given sound advice that students are ignoring. Usually, advice was given, but not understood. Additionally, the advice may be too general to be helpful. Students may wish to ask what constitutes a stronger argument, but are reluctant to do so. Starke-Meyerring (2011) writes, "With writing beneath the cloak of normalcy, questions about writing—about knowledge production—becomes risky business" (p. 86). Frequently students preface important questions with, "This may be a stupid question." Starke-Meyerring adds, "Students experience a sense of being left in the dark, learning by trial and error, or by chance" (p. 85). Many assume their peers understand everything and they blame themselves for not being smart enough. They need help but do know the questions to ask to get it, and many are afraid to ask. There really are no stupid questions, and there is a good chance many peers have the same questions. Students need to ask, and ask again, to uncover tacit knowledge.

Students often complain that their supervisor gives inconsistent advice. During one meeting, she or he may suggest a theory, a source, or a direction, only to reverse the decision during next meeting. To keep this to a minimum, students can gently remind the supervisor of the requested changes by summarizing the proposed changes in a cover letter accompanying the revised draft. Explain how each point was addressed in the text. This is the same strategy one would use when submitting revisions for a paper that is accepted with modifications for publication. The author must tell the editor how the changes were made. If the student disagrees with the supervisor's comments, he or she should give a good rationale for ignoring them.

When supervisors spend time correcting texts, pay close attention to the corrections. One supervisor I interviewed laughed and said he spends hours reading and commenting on papers. His students check "accept" to all comments and resubmit the paper ten minutes later. The supervisor's comments not only correct the student's research, but provide clues to the academic language of the discipline.

After submitting a draft to the supervisor, do not, under any circumstances, continue to work on the same draft. One supervisor I interviewed recounted an instance where he spent hours reading and commenting on a draft. When he returned it to the student, the student said he reworked it and had taken another direction. The supervisor said this was "a horrible waste of my time." One can surmise that the next time this student submits a draft far less investment will be made reading and commenting on it. Once a draft is submitted, work on another section of the thesis. Update the literature review.

Conclusion

Intelligence, skill, and innate talent helps, but persistence is needed to finish a thesis. Establishing a regular writing schedule with clear deadlines replicates coursework. It breaks the mammoth job of writing a thesis into manageable parts and helps to put the task of writing a thesis into perspective. At its most basic level, the thesis is an academic exercise that demonstrates the capacity to carry out research. It is a take home, open book exam. The thesis demonstrates the ability to systematically gather and analyze date. A completed thesis tells a cohesive story of that research.

CHAPTER 11

DEALING WITH STUDENT-SUPERVISOR PROBLEMS

INTRODUCTION

Not all relationships work out as planned. Considering the stress graduate students experience and the amount of time it takes for some to complete a thesis, it is not surprising that some student–supervisor relationships deteriorate. Relationships break down for a number of reasons though supervisors and students disagree on the cause. Graduate students cite reasons such as bad advising (Gardner, 2008), lack of interaction, trust, emotional support (Golde, 2005), and a mismatch in styles (Lee, 2007). Gardner's (2008) study on student attrition found that faculty members put the blame solely on the students who left. Faculty members cited students' lack of ability, drive, or motivation as reasons they were not successful. Some believed the student should not have come to the university in the first place. This resonated with one supervisor I interviewed who said her department routinely accepted students of poor quality.

Issues of power imbalance exist in the academy, and even in the most collegial graduate student and supervisor relationships. University structures give supervisors powers over the students they supervise. In addition to help with their theses, students need numerous letters of reference from their supervisors. Some students are employees of their supervisors, and are dependent on them for their income. When faced with a deteriorating or unworkable student–supervisor relationship, what are the student's options?

Addressing Problems with Your Supervisor

Changing supervisors may be considered, but that should be a last resort. First, meet with the supervisor to attempt to resolve problems before they escalate. Before meeting with the supervisor, discuss the problems with a trusted friend to articulate the problem. Students may not feel supported by their supervisor, but they need to be clear about what this means. In one case, a student did not feel supported by the supervisor because the supervisor elected to attend another student's presentation at a conference but not hers. Another waited four months to receive feedback. Next, consider what specific actions are needed to resolve the problem. As an associate dean of students, I occasionally met with students who demanded, "something be done" about a particular situation. When asked what actions might remedy the situation, they often said, "Fire the professor." One student wanted to expose the professor to the greater university as a bad supervisor. This won't work and in many cases, there is simply no remedy for bad supervision.

Most universities have graduate supervision guidelines. Although these are usually policy statements or suggested best practices, they can give an indication of what the university deems as the supervisor's roles and responsibilities. Guidelines also indicate the student's responsibilities. Guidelines differ among universities. Some guidelines fill an extensive book while others are a few pages. It is good to become familiar with the guidelines before problems arise. However, it is naïve to believe that students have the power to force supervisors to carry out their duties. Even if university guidelines clearly state it is the supervisor who is responsible for reading a draft for publication, pointing this out will not improve the situation. I reiterate that supervision is a voluntary act for faculty.

Getting Effective Feedback from Your Supervisor

Students need feedback from their supervisors to keep the research moving and ensure it is moving in the right direction. There are times when students need more input than others. Students will need to see their supervisor when developing their proposal and at the start of their data analysis. As the research progresses, students should work to become independent researchers.

It is acceptable to ask when a supervisor expects to provide feedback. Most guidelines use the word "timely," but few define what this means. How fast can the student expect a reply? Within an hour, a day, or a week? Consider the peak times for the supervisor. Is there a major grant deadline? Does the professor have midterm or final papers to mark? Is this the time other students are rushing to meet the deadlines to defend their theses? Does the supervisor respond to emails on weekends and evening? If not, send the questions in the morning or on Monday when the professor will read and respond. Otherwise, the email may be buried under other emails.

Receiving encouraging and motivating feedback goes a long way to help students reach their goal. Some supervisors give back news, but little praise. I have a memory of an instructor I had as a student who wrote particularly nasty comments on student papers. I went to his office to complain. When asked directly what I wanted, I told him I wanted some positive feedback to balance the negative comments. I still recall his words, "Oh, so you want me to be patronizing?" Incidentally, I later submitted an abstract of the paper to a conference and it was accepted. Students should not take this feedback as a personal attack, though it may certainly feel like it is. It is possible that supervisors are not aware of the tone of their feedback. Respond to any feedback in writing, quoting what needs corrected. Perhaps if these supervisors routinely read their remarks, they will consider tempering them.

Fortunately, some students manage to write a thesis despite their supervisor. They evaluate their needs and find alternative sources to meet them. Committee members can provide some help but most will be reluctant to step into the supervisor's role. Peer groups, communities of practice, and friends can help. Many universities offer graduate workshops that provide information on grant writing, career searches, and other services.

Making a Formal Complaint

If problems cannot be resolved with the supervisor, the student needs to be aware of the university's chain of command. A well-written letter to the university president will be passed down the line, usually ending on the desk of the graduate program director. To save time, it is best to start there. The GPD should know the policies and procedures for changing supervisors. They may know what is reasonable to ask of a supervisor and what is reasonable to expect. Graduate program directors can usually be trusted to hold your discussion in confidence. If the GPD cannot help, the next step is to seek help from the department chair. Finally, seek help from the school of graduate studies' director of student services or associate dean of students. Complaints should clearly indicate the nature of the problem and the action needed to remedy the problem. It is within the student's prerogative to ask to meet the supervisor with another member of the faculty present. Usually this faculty member would be the GPD or department chair. Students who make a strong case of neglect or abuse will be treated with more attention. For example, students who claim their supervisor cancelled their last four meetings, and show documentation in emails have a strong case for action.

Changing Supervisors

Not all problems can be resolved and not everyone is willing to work toward a resolution. If the student–supervisor relationship is beyond reconciliation, what is the best way to end the supervisory relationship? What are the costs involved in changing supervisors? What are the benefits? How does a student go about finding another supervisor? I posed these questions to many supervisors. Some were nonchalant and recalled experiences where they and a student mutually agreed they were not the best person to supervise. In one example, the student's research interests changed and both felt a colleague was better suited for the task. However, others recounted instances of students switching supervisors, saying they felt betrayed. A key factor in this discussion was how much supervisors felt they had invested in the student's progress. Supervisors who believed to have invested little in terms of money and time were open to students changing supervisors. Those who perceived that they had given special attention or gone above and beyond the call of duty for the student were resentful and hurt. This suggests that students should act early rather than continue when the relationship is not going well.

Disciplinary differences should be factored into decisions to change supervisors. In the social sciences and humanities, supervisors typically provide less funding for students and have less reliance on them for their research, than do those in science and engineering. Among the supervisors whom I spoke to, those who had provided funding for students, and made place for them in labs, were more concerned when students planned to change supervisors. In addition, supervisors were less likely too accept a student who left another faculty member's lab. Students who have been accepted into programs on the condition of working with specific supervisors and rely on them for funding and research space will have a much harder time finding another supervisor than will students in the social sciences and humanities. It should also be noted that if a student changes supervisors, it is also likely the advisory committee will change as well.

Among those I interviewed, there was little agreement about the wisdom of changing supervisors, but one thing is clear: changing supervisors slows student progress. Time lost depends on where the student is in the thesis. Students at the proposal stage lose less than students who have written a complete draft of the thesis. Changing supervisors can require students to write a new proposal, with a new topic and methodology. For the masters student, most agreed it was not worth the time and effort to change. They held that most masters students should persist for a year, even with a less than satisfactory supervisor relationship.

Golde's (2005) research on student attrition found that a number of students elect to transfer to another university rather than change supervisors in their university. According to Golde, students who elected to change schools made more informed choices about their new supervisor and this allowed them to "start over with a clean slate" (p. 687). However, it can also require students to take additional courses and repeat comprehensive exams. In some cases, students may lose government funding.

This bleak discussion might give the impression one should never change supervisors. However, in some cases the benefits can outweigh the costs. This was true for a student I call Joseph. After working two years with a supervisor, and writing three chapters for his thesis, their relationship came to a mutual halt. There was, among other issues, a disagreement over how much feedback a supervisor should provide. Joseph asked that his supervisor read and comment on papers for publication. The supervisor expressed that his job was to supervise the thesis. Lee (2007) might label the supervisory style as "benign neglect" (p. 685). There was a mismatch of the student's needs and the supervisor's willingness to attend to those needs. After several unproductive meetings, they independently agreed to dissolve the relationship. Joseph was able to find a new supervisor, but this supervisor was not an expert on the original topic and research method. The new supervisor required Joseph to rewrite his proposal. Despite the time lost in starting over, Joseph was able to write and defend his thesis in two additional years. And with his supervisor's support, he was able to publish. The time lost in starting over was gained in self-confidence and supervisor support. Starting over or redoing work may be a better option than dropping out. If students change supervisors, they should give credit to the original supervisor for his or her contribution to the research and for any financial support.

Before initiating a change in supervisors, students should know their rights and ascertain if another faculty member is willing to serve. They should also weigh the cost. For example, students at my university are given only four months to secure a new supervisor, after which they will be withdrawn from their program. Other universities may require the department chair to assign another faculty member to the supervisory role provided he or she is qualified to supervise the research.

Sexual Harassment, Racism, Homophobia, and Discrimination

Research indicates between one quarter and one third of all female university and college students face sexual harassment (Smeby, 2000). Certainly, harassment is not something that happens only to women and as we know, it is a vastly underreported crime. Most universities have policies to deal with sexual and other forms of harassment, but these are not always effective and in some instances, the student's complaint is not given the attention it deserves. This was recently demonstrated in an advice column where an anonymous writer asked Alice Huang (2015) for advice concerning her supervisor looking down her blouse. Huang replied,

As long as your adviser does not move on to other advances, I suggest you put up with it, with good humor if you can. Just make sure that he is listening to you and your ideas, taking in the results you are presenting, and taking your science seriously. His attention on your chest may be unwelcome, but you need his attention on your science and his best advice. (n.p.)[1]

Huang added that this sort of behavior was common in the workplace. This was confirmed by Nobel laureate Tim Hunt's "trouble with girls in the lab" speech. "You fall in love with them, they fall in love with you, and when you criticize them, they cry" (quoted in Clatterbuck Soper, 2015).

Unfortunately, some professors who agree to supervise lack adequate social and academic skills needed to effectively mentor graduate students. It bears repeating that professors are rarely trained to take on the demanding role of supervisor and many would not avail themselves to such support if it existed. Moreover, there is little consequence for bad supervision. Golde, Bueschel, Jones, and Walker (2006) write, "More insidiously, the student is completely dependent on the faculty advisor, who, through ignorance, convention, or malice abuses or exploits the student" (p. 5). They claim that a "culture of privacy" means that faculty members and departmental leaders seldom intervene on behalf of the student leaving the student with little recourse (p. 5).

Some, like Huang, may advise students to ignore problems, get their degree, and move on, noting the costs of complaining are too high. I disagree. No student should have to endure harassment or psychological abuse to obtain a graduate degree. Sexism, racism, homophobia, and forms of discrimination are unacceptable and should be brought to the university's attention. The academy is not above the law, nor is a faculty member exempt from civil behavior. It is the university's responsibility to provide a safe, welcoming environment for all students. Operating under a culture of privacy allows the abuse to continue.

NOTE

[1] *Science* removed the column and issued an apology.

CHAPTER 12

DEFENDING THE THESIS

INTRODUCTION

Often referred to as a rite of passage, the defense is a ritual that marks the transition from student to a full member of the academic tribe. The purpose of the defense is not made clear to students. Is it an exam, where one passes or fails, or is it a celebratory event to publicly unveil years of solitary work? Defenses cause much anxiety for students who approach them because they are unsure if they will pass and this failure will be announced publicly. "Defense" is an unfortunate word to describe this event as it suggests defensiveness, which students need not feel. Wellington (2010) notes that supervisors are not helpful in preparing students for their defense, and often revert back to their own defense for advice. This chapter provides an inside view of the defense process to let students know what to expect to alleviate some of the stress that comes with the ritual.

Each country, university, and program lends specifics to the ritual, but most involve peer review. Once the supervisor, and in some cases the thesis committee, deems the thesis to be ready to defend, the student submits it to the school of graduate studies or the university's thesis office. Some universities permit students to submit their thesis without their supervisor's approval, but this is highly discouraged. The supervisor has experience in this matter and probably makes this decision in the student's best interest. In any case, the thesis is a reflection of the supervisor, the department, and the university and no supervisor wants to damage her or his reputation by sending a subpar thesis to a colleague from another department or university (Mullins & Kiley, 2002).

The defense begins with examiners reading and commenting on the thesis. For master's students, one or two faculty members from their home department independently read the thesis and provide written comments. They may ask for minor or major revisions. Minor revisions are completed at the discretion of the supervisor, whereas major revisions usually mean the thesis will be returned to the examiners for a second reading after the student has made the required changes. Oral defenses, if required, usually involve the student meeting with their thesis committee. However, some master's programs involve externals to the department, but usually not to the university.

Doctoral defenses in North America typically involve at least five examiners, who form the examining committee. In some cases, the committee consists of thesis committee members, the supervisor, and one or more external examiners. Some universities do not permit the supervisor to be part of the examining committee. External examiners are subject experts from other universities or other departments within the university and are expected to be at "arms length," having neither collaborated with the supervisor or student. Usually, if there are several external examiners at least one external examiner is from the student's university, but from outside their department. This "internal external" may have some knowledge of topic or method and serves a gate-keeping role, ensuring a consistent thesis quality across the university. Many universities in the United States do not require examiners external to the university. Supervisors and thesis committee members may suggest names of individuals to serve as examiners. In some departments, a graduate committee approves the examiners. Students have little input in these decisions, but should be part of the discussion.

What Is the "Good Enough" Thesis?

How do examiners judge theses? What criteria are important to them? While the answer differs for each examiner, most start reading in hopes the thesis will be good or at least good enough to pass. Some read the introductory chapter, and continue to read as one would read a novel. Others start by checking the references. Some are careful readers, while others read for overall impressions. Some scrutinize specific chapters more closely than others, such as the methodology or the analysis. And, I suspect, some read only the abstract. Mullins and Kiley (2002) interviewed 30 experienced thesis examiners to determine their criteria and expected level of student achievement in completed doctoral theses. A majority of those interviewed said that first impressions were important, and influenced how they judged the thesis. This impression was usually formed by the second or third chapter, and "often by the end of the literature review" (p. 377).

Examiners cited two factors as being particularly problematic: sloppiness and inconsistency. Sloppiness was defined as "typographical errors, or mistakes in calculations, referencing and footnotes" (Mullins & Kiley, 2002, p. 378). Examiners regarded these mistakes as red flags, signaling a larger problem. Sloppiness might mean the student was in a hurry to finish the thesis and may have submitted a first draft. If the writing was careless, the examiners thought the student's reasoning might be careless as well. Did the student take time to analyze the data, or was the thesis speculative? Would greater insights have surfaced in later drafts? Typographical errors and a lack of attention to details always detract from an otherwise good thesis and causes examiners to "flip" from positive to negative. As one examiner stated, "Once flipped (and I am aware of this happening), I am irritated and have to work very hard at overcoming this irritation and not letting it influence my view of the thesis, although this is not easy" (p. 378). Missing and incorrect citations signaled a larger problem of possible plagiarism. Locating sources after the thesis has been submitted is time consuming and can be avoided if citation is done habitually.

The second issue was that of inconsistency. Did the student actually do what he or she set out to do? Was the thesis coherent? Did the literature inform the findings? Did the student answer the research question? Some theses were the result of several years work, and early chapters may not have reflected the research. The findings might have suggested different literature than what was provided in the literature review. The writing style may have been inconsistent. These problems occur when students write early chapters but do not revisit them before submitting. Students who write theses with their publications should take care to bring the publications into a cohesive document. The publications must be linked theoretically and together demonstrate a substantial contribution to knowledge.

Good theses, on the other hand, were coherent, and had a well structured argument. Reflection was also mentioned as a characteristic of a good thesis. An outstanding thesis was described as "artful," both exciting and sparkling. However, it is helpful to remember as one examiner noted, "A Ph.D. is three years of solid work, not a Nobel Prize" (Mullin & Kiley, 2002, p. 369).

The examiners are given a specific amount of time, usually between six and eight weeks, to read the thesis and submit a written report. Some universities allow students or supervisors access to the report but others do not. If a majority of the examining committee agrees the thesis is of a sufficient quality to defend, then an oral examination will take place. If the examining committee finds significant gaps, or believe the thesis to be poorly written, the oral examination can be cancelled. The student must make all corrections and resubmit the thesis to the supervisor, who restarts the process.

What Does an Oral Examination Entail?

Oral examinations are the norm in North America. Only a few Australian universities hold oral examinations, and only at the request of one of the examiners. In the UK, the term "viva" is used rather than "defense". Defenses differ from university to university, and from program to program. For some, they are public performances, with the academic community and friends in attendance. Others are private affairs, including only a student audience, or only the student and the examining committee.

If the university permits it, the best way to prepare is to attend as many others as is possible, starting in the first year of study. If students attend only one, they may think it to be typical, when it was not. They will be either too casual or too worried. Defenses can be lively affairs, well attended by family and friends offering support to the student. Or, they can involve the student sitting alone at one side of long table, facing five stern looking examiners. Students can take careful note how other students present their research and what kinds of questions are asked.

Usually, a doctoral defense has two components: a timed presentation by the student and a question period. Students should prepare for the defense presentation as they would an important conference presentation. It should be rehearsed and take the time allotted, not more and not less. This is usually around 30 minutes. Very short presentations diminish the contribution of the research, while those that drag on indicate the student is not able to reflect on the over all research process. These students walk the audience though every detail of the thesis but miss the major contributions. In some cases, the chair of the examination will stop the overtime presentation before the student gets to the conclusion.

The presentation is intended to demonstrate public speaking skills and ensure the examiners that the student did the work. Students who cannot explain their analysis will face tough questions later. Technology allows for a wider number of examiners and increasingly, external examiners attend the oral defense remotely. Students with examiners attending remotely should prepare the presentation and send it to the examiners in advance of the defense. When presenting, students should periodically check that the examiner is on the same slide or page.

Very early in the presentation, students should clearly state the thesis's original contribution to knowledge and highlight the contributions the thesis makes to the field. This statement must be balanced in telling what the thesis does but without overstating the contribution.

Immediately after presentation concludes, committee members launch into their questions. The question period can take many forms. They can follow a round table format, starting with the external examiner, and giving the last question to the supervisor, if they permitted to attend. Or, they can be open discussions with dialogue, or fights, between members of the examining committee. It is important to remember that the questions are on one hand directed to the student, but are also a display of the examiners' competence for their colleagues. Their questions are in many ways intended to make them look good in front of their peers. No examiner wants to ask a stupid or obvious question.

Oral defenses are performances and students may encounter people playing various roles. Some appear to use the defense to impress the examining panel, and anyone who attends, with their own knowledge. The rambling examiner goes on and on, but never asks a question. He or she is thinking aloud, or musing from topic to topic, and arrives, after a long aside, at a comment that resembles a question. This is rarely in the form of a question, but a request to "elaborate on." The forensic investigator is the opposite of the rambler. He or she asks specific questions about passages or even words. They often preface their question with, "On page 243, paragraph two, you use the word…" They have usually prepared twenty or thirty questions prior to the defense.

Examiners external to the department often attempt to make links with the student's thesis and their own research, regardless of how removed it is. Recently, a student, defending a thesis about Byzantine icons, was asked to make a connection with puppetry. Fortunately, this student knew his subject well and managed to answer the question. And, of course, there are examiners who, frankly, did not read the thesis. Invariably, they ask a question to which the student devoted two chapters.

Wellington (2010) and Chen (2011) posit that the majority of questions can be predicted. They usually pertain to motivation, researcher position, theory, the literature review, methodology, and generalizability, or applicability. They identify over fifty questions routinely asked at defenses. These questions are useful for mock defenses. A general question, for example, might ask how the student arrived at the thesis topic. Examples of analysis questions are, "Why did you analyze the data in this way? What would be some alternative ways?" (p. 103). The defending student should be able to identify his or her coding system and describe the audit trail. Chen (2011) recommends that students conduct a background check on examiners' research. Their research holds clues as to the subject, theories, and methodology questions they may ask.

When addressing questions, students should strive to make examiners feel good about their question. Taking a moment to reflect before answering does this. Some respond immediately with the phrase, "Good question." However, students should follow by explaining why this is the case. Students are anxious to answer the question, and have the tendency to interrupt the rambler to address the first thing than resembles a question. However, the examiner is only taking a breath and more is to follow. Students should wait until the examiner settles back in his or her chair and then attempt to compose a question. It is acceptable to ask for clarification about a question before answering. Students should also keep notes, writing each question. No matter what is asked, students should never argue with the examiner or attempt to correct the examiner's (mis)understanding. However, some examiners enjoy playing the devil's advocate and students should defend their work.

After at least two rounds of questions, the chair will confirm that everyone is satisfied and no more questions will be asked. The chair either asks visitors and the student to leave the room, or the committee leaves to deliberate. A vote is taken as to whether or not the thesis has passed, and if any revisions are required. Generally, the decision is taken by a majority vote, but not all members of the examining committee have the same impact on the decision. More importance is given to examiners external to the university. However, any problems should have been indicated in the external's report prior to the defense. Additionally, a vote is taken to determine if the student passed the oral defense.

The thesis can be accepted "as is," or with minor revisions. Some universities regard the need for major revisions as not passing while other consider it to be accepted, conditionally. Major revisions will mean the supervisor must prove to the committee that the changes have been met. Sometimes, the examining committee must read the thesis a second time. The thought of having to read a thesis a second time prevents many theses from being judged in this category.

Students want to do more than pass their defense. They want to feel challenged and confident they met the challenge. They want to know experts in their field engaged with their work. Most students pass their exams, but not everyone recalls their defense as a positive experience. Using a sports metaphor, the best defense is a good offense, which means submitting a carefully researched and well-written thesis, and making an organized presentation.

After the defense, many students experience a well-deserved sense of elation and accomplishment. Others, however, may be surprised to discover they feel sad. Their experience may be similar to a post-partum depression. For others, the experience is like the break-up of a close relationship. Many, who have been students for a greater portion of their adult life, experience a loss of identity. Additionally, some may feel a loss of purpose. Those who dreamed of the day they had no thesis to write now find a void. There may be a sense of "so what" or "now what?"

It is important to recognize that these feelings are a normal part of the journey, and that they will pass. Writing and defending a thesis is life transforming and it takes time to forge a new identity and set new goals. Be confident that the skills needed to research and write a thesis transfer to all aspects of life. The passion and curiosity that led to pursuing a graduate degree will return. Congratulations on achieving this milestone.

REFERENCES

Abasi, A., & Graves, B. (2008). Academic literacy and plagiarism: Conversations with international graduate students and disciplinary professors. *Journal of English for Academic Purposes, 7*, 221–233. doi:10.1016/j.jeap.2008.10.010

American Art Therapy Association. (2013). *What is art therapy?* Retrieved from www.arttherapy.org/upload/whatisarttherapy.pdf

APA Science Student Council. (2006). *A graduate student's guide to determining authorship credit and authorship order.* Retrieved from www.apa.org/science/leadership/students/authorship-paper.pdf

Barone, T., & Eisner, E. (2012). *Arts based research.* Thousand Oaks, CA: Sage.

Barrett, T. (1990). *Criticizing photographs: An introduction to understanding images.* Mountain View, CA: Mayfield Publishing Company.

Barrett, T. (2000). *Criticizing art: Understanding the contemporary.* New York, NY: McGraw Hill.

Baumeister, R., & Leary, M. (1997). Writing narrative literature reviews. *Review of General Psychology, 1*(3), 311–320. Retrieved from http://dx.doi.org/10.1037/1089-2680.1.3.311

Beam, G. (2012). *The problem with survey research.* Piscataway, NJ: Transaction Publishers.

Biklen, S. K., & Casella, R. (2007). *A practical guide to the qualitative dissertation.* New York, NY & London: Teachers College Press.

Billig, M. (2013). *Learn to write badly: How to succeed in the social sciences.* Cambridge: Cambridge University Press.

Blackstone, M., Given, L., Lévy, J., McGinn, M., O'Neill, P., Palys, T., & van den Hoonaard, W. (2008). *Research involving creative practices: A chapter for the inclusion in the TCPS.* Retrieved from http://www.pre.ethics.gc.ca/eng/archives/policypolitique/reports-rapports/ricp-ripc/

Bolker, J. (1998). *Writing your thesis in fifteen minutes a day: A guide to starting, revising, and finishing your doctoral thesis.* New York, NY: Owl Books.

Booth, A., Papaioannou, D., & Sutton, A. (2012). *Systematic approaches to a successful literature review.* Los Angeles, CA: Sage.

Bourke, N., & Neilsen, P. (2004). The problem of the exegesis in creative writing higher degrees. *TEXT Special Issue, 3.* Retrieved from http://www.griffith.edu.au/school/art/text

Bowen, D. H., Greene, J. P., & Kisida, B. (2013). Learning to think critically: A visual art experiment. *Educational Researcher, 43*(1), 37–44. doi:10.3102/0013189x13512675

Boydell, K. M., Volpe, T., Cox, S., Katz, A., Dow, R., Brunger, F., … Wong, L. (2011). Ethical challenges in arts-based health research. *The International Journal of Creative Arts in Interdisciplinary Practice, 11*, 1–17. Retrieved from www.ijcaip.com/archives/IJCAIP-11-paper1.pdf

Brewer, E. W., & Kuhn, J. (2010). Causal-comparative design. In N. Salkind (Ed.), *Encyclopedia of research design* (pp. 125–131). Thousand Oaks, CA: Sage. doi:http://dx.doi.org/10.4135/9781412961288

Byers, V. T., Smith, R. N., Hwang, E., Angrove, K. E., Chandler, J. I., Christian, K. M., … McAlster-Shields, L. (2014). Survival strategies: Doctoral student's perceptions of challenges and coping methods. *International Journal of Doctoral Studies, 9*, 109–136. Retrieved from http://ijds.org/Volume9/IJDSv9p109-136Byers0384.pdf

Canadian Institute of Health Research, Natural Science and Engineering Research Council of Canada, and Social Sciences and Humanities Research Council of Canada. (2014). *Tri-council policy statement: Ethical conduct for research involving humans.* Retrieved from http://www.pre.ethics.gc.ca/eng/policy-politique/initiatives/tcps2-eptc2/Default/

Carter, S. M., & Little, M. (2007). Justifying knowledge, justifying method, taking action: Epistemologies, methodologies, and methods in qualitative research. *Qualitative Health Researcher, 17*(10), 1316–1328. doi:10.1177/1049732307306927

Chapman, O., & Sawchuk, K. (2012). Research-creation: Intervention, analysis and "family resemblances." Special Issue on Media Arts Revisited. *Canadian Journal of Communication, 37*(1), 5–26. Retrieved from http://www.cjconline.ca/index.php/journal/article/view/2489

Chapman, V. L., & Sork, T. (2001). Confessing regulation or telling secrets? Opening up the conversation on graduate supervision. *Adult Education Quarterly, 51*(2), 94–107. Retrieved from http://dx.doi.org/10.1177/07417136010512002

Charmaz, K. (2006). *Constructing grounded theory: A practical guide through qualitative analysis.* Thousand Oaks, CA: Sage.

Chase, S. (2011). Narrative inquiry: Still a field in the making. In N. Denzin & Y. Lincoln (Eds.), *The Sage handbook of qualitative research* (pp. 421–434). Los Angeles, CA: Sage.

Chen, S. (2011). Making sense of the doctoral dissertation defense: A student-experience-based perspective. In L. McAlpine & C. Amundsen (Eds.), *Doctoral education: Research-based strategies for doctoral students, supervisors and administrators* (pp. 97–114). Dordrecht: Springer.

Chenail, R. (2008). "But is it research?": A review of Patricia Leavy's *Method meets art: Art-based research practice. The Weekly Qualitative Report, 1*(2), 7–12. Retrieved from http://www.nova.edu/ssss/QR/WQR/leavy.pdf

Chilton, G., & Leavy, P. (2015). Arts-based research practice: Merging social research and creative arts. In P. Leavy (Ed.), *The Oxford handbook of qualitative research* (pp. 403–422). New York, NY: Oxford University Press.

Clance, P., & Imes, S. (1978). The imposter phenomenon in high achieving women: Dynamics and therapeutic intervention. *Psychotherapy: Theory, Research & Practice, 15*(3), 241–247. Retrieved from http://dx.doi.org/10.1037/h0086006

Clatterbuck Soper, S. (2015, June 18). What it's like as a 'girl' in the lab. *The New York Times.* Retrieved from http://www.nytimes.com/2015/06/18/opinion/whatitslikeasagirlinthelab.html?_r=0

Clausen, K. (2012). The ends and the mean-spirited in action research: An editorial. *Canadian Journal of Action Research, 13*(2), 1–2. Retrieved from http://cjar.nipissingu.ca/index.php/cjar/article/view/34

COPE: Committee on Publication Ethics. (2014). *What constitutes authorship?* COPE discussion document. Retrieved from http://publicationethics.org/resources/discussiondocuments

Cox, S., Drew, S., Guilleman, M., Howell, C., Warr, D., & Waycott, J. (2014). *Guidelines for ethical visual research methods.* Melbourne: The University of Melbourne. Retrieved from artshealthnetwork.ca/ahnc/ethical_visual_research_methods-web.pdf

Creswell, J. W. (2013). *Qualitative inquiry & research design: Choosing among five traditions.* Thousand Oaks, CA: Sage.

Crombie, I., & Davies, H. (2009). What is meta-analysis? *Evidence Based Medicine.* Retrieved from www.whatisseries.co.uk

Delamont, S., Parry, O., & Atkinson, P. (1998). Creating a delicate balance: The doctoral supervisor's dilemmas. *Teaching in Higher Education, 3*(2), 157–172. Retrieved from http://dx.doi.org/10.1080/1356215980030203

Denzin, N. K., & Lincoln, Y. S. (2011). Introduction: The discipline and practice of qualitative research. In N. Denzin & Y. Lincoln (Eds.), *The Sage handbook of qualitative research* (pp. 1–20). Los Angeles, CA: Sage.

Donmoyer, R., Eisner, E., & Gardner, H. (1996). *Can a novel be a dissertation?* American Educational Research Association Annual Meeting, New York, NY.

Donovan, S. (2007). The importance of resubmitting rejected papers. *Journal of Scholarly Publishing, 38*(3), 151–155.

Dunlop, R. (1999). Boundary bay: A novel as educational research (Unpublished doctoral dissertation). The University of British Columbia, Vancouver. Retrieved from https://circle.ubc.ca/handle/2429/9957

Dunne, C. (2011). The place of the literature review in grounded theory research. *International Journal of Social Research Methodology, 14*(2), 111–124. doi:10.1080/13645579.2010.494930

Eckel, E. J. (2010). A reflection on plagiarism, patchwriting, and the engineering master's thesis. *Issues in Science and Technology Librarianship, 62*(9). doi:10.5062/F4NC5Z42

Ellis, C. (2007). Telling secrets, revealing lives: Relational ethics in research with intimate others. *Qualitative Inquiry, 13*(1), 3–29. doi:10.1177/1077800406294947

Fanghanel, J. (2009). The role of ideology in shaping academics' conception of their discipline. *Teaching in Higher Education, 14*(5), 565–577. Retrieved from http://dx.doi.org/10.1080/13562510903186790

Felder, P., & Barker, M. (2013). Extending Bell's concept of interest convergence: A framework for understanding the African American doctoral student experience. *International Journal of Doctoral Studies, 8*, 1–20. Retrieved from http://ijds.org/Volume8/IJDSv8p001-020Felder0384.pdf

Felder, P., Stevenson, H., & Gasman, M. (2014). Understanding race in doctoral student socialization. *International Journal of Doctoral Studies, 9*, 21–42. Retrieved from http://ijds.org/Volume9/IJDSv9p021-042Felder0323.pdf

Fenge, L. (2009). Professional doctorates—A better route for researching professionals. *Social Work Education, 28*(2), 165–167. doi:10.1080/02615470701865733

Fink, A. (2010). *Conducting research literature reviews from the Internet to paper.* Los Angeles, CA: Sage.

Furco, A., & Moely, B. (2012). Using learning communities to build faculty support for pedagogical innovation: A multi-campus study. *The Journal of Higher Education, 83*(1), 128–153. doi:10.1353/jhe.2012.0006

Garber, J. (2008). Face validity. In P. Lavrakas (Ed.), *Encyclopedia of survey research methods* (pp. 471–474). Thousand Oaks, CA: Sage. doi:http://dx.doi.org/10.4135/9781412963947

Gardner, S. (2008). Student and faculty attributions of attrition in high and low completing doctoral programs in the United States. *Higher Education, 58*, 97–112. Retrieved from http://dx.doi.org/10.1007/s10734-008-9184-7

Garfield, E. (2007). The evolution of the scientific citation index. *International Microbiology, 10*, 65–69. Retrieved from http://dx.doi.org/10.2436/20.1501.01.10

Given, L. (2008). *The Sage encyclopedia of qualitative methods.* Thousand Oaks: CA: Sage.

Glaser, B. G. (1998). *Doing grounded theory: Issues and discussions.* Mill Valley, CA: Sociology Press.

Glaser, B. G., & Strauss, A. (1967). *Discovery of grounded theory.* Chicago, IL: Aldine.

Golde, C. (2005). The role of the department and discipline in doctoral student attrition: Lessons from four departments. *The Journal of Higher Education, 76*(6), 669–700. Retrieved from http://www.jstor.org/stable/3838782

Golde, C., Bueschel, A. C., Jones, L., & Walker, G. E. (2006). *Apprenticeship and intellectual community: Lessons from the Carnegie initiative on the doctorate.* Retrieved from http://drupal-dev.ilr.cornell.edu

Gu, Q., & Brooks, J. (2008). Beyond the accusation of plagiarism. *System, 36*, 337–352. doi:10.1016/j.system.2008.01.004

Haas, T. N. (2014). How to avoid common presentation mistakes at international conferences. *International Engineering Science and Innovation Technology (IJESIT), 3*(4). Retrieved from https://www.google.ca/?gws_rd=ssl#q=how+to+avoid+common+presentation+mistakes+haas+trevor

Harriman, S., & Patel, J. (2014). The ethics and editorial challenges of internet-based research. *BMC Medicine, 12*, 124. doi:10.1186/s12916-014-0124-3

Hayes, N., & Introna, L. (2005). Cultural values, plagiarism, and fairness: When plagiarism gets in the way of learning. *Ethics & Behavior, 15*(3), 213–231. Retrieved from http://dx.doi.org/10.1207/s15327019eb1503_2

Herr, K., & Anderson, G. (2015). *The action research dissertation.* Los Angeles, CA: Sage.

Hirsh, M. (2010). *The liberators: America's witnesses to the Holocaust.* New York, NY: Penguin Random House.

Holbrook, A., Bourke, S., Fairbairn, H., & Lovat, T. (2007). Examiner comments on the literature review in Ph.D. theses. *Studies in Higher Education, 32*(3), 337–356. Retrieved from http://dx.doi.org/10.1080/03075070701346899

Holm, G. (2015). Photography as a research method. In P. Leavy (Ed.), *The Oxford handbook of qualitative research* (pp. 380–402.) New York, NY: Oxford University Press.

Hopkins, W. G. (2000). Quantitative research design. *Sportscience, 4*(1). Retrieved from http://sportsci.org/jour/0001/wghdesign.html

Howard, R. (1993). A plagiarism pentimento. *Journal of Teaching Writing, 11*(3), 233–246. Retrieved from http://eric.ed.gov/?id=EJ475663

Howard, R., Serviss, T., & Rodrique, T. (2010). Writing from sources, writing from sentences. *Writing Pedagogy, 2*(2), 177–192.

Huang, A. (2015, June 1). Help! My advisor won't stop looking down my shirt. *Science.* Retrieved from http://sciencecareers.sciencemag.org/career_magazine/previous_issues/articles/2015_06_01/caredit.a1500140

Iacovetta, F., & Taylor-Ladd, M. (2010). *Becoming a historian: A Canadian manual.* Canadian Historical Association, the Canadian Committee on Women's History, the AHA Committee on Women Historians, and the American Historical Association. Retrieved from https://www.google.ca/?gws_rd=ssl#q=iacovetta+taylor+ladd+conference+circuit

Jacob, M. J. (2014). *Learning to make, making to learn comics creation: The intrinsic educational qualities contained within comics and their formation* (Masters thesis). Concordia University, Québec. Retrieved from http://spectrum.library.concordia.ca/978974/

James, R., & Baldwin, G. (1999). *Eleven practices of effective postgraduate supervisors.* Victoria, Australia: University of Melbourne. Retrieved from http://www.cshe.unimelb.edu.au/pdfs/11practices.pdf

Janesick, V. (2015). Oral history interviewing: Issues and possibilities. In P. Leavy (Ed.), *The Oxford handbook of qualitative research* (pp. 300–314) New York, NY: Oxford University Press.

Jesson, J., Matheson, L., & Lacey, F. (2011). *Doing your literature review: Traditional and systematic techniques.* London: Sage Publications Ltd.

Johnson, B., & Christensen, L. B. (2013). *Educational research: Quantitative, qualitative, and mixed approaches.* Thousand Oaks, CA: Sage.

Kamler, B., & Thomson, P. (2006). *Helping doctoral students write: Pedagogies for supervision.* London & New York, NY: Routledge.

Kiley, M. (2009). Identifying threshold concepts and proposing strategies to support doctoral candidates. *Innovations in Education and Teaching International, 46*(3), 293–304. doi:10.1080/14703290903069001

Kincheloe, J., LcLauren, P., & Steinberg, S. (2011). Critical pedagogy and qualitative research: Moving to the bricolage. In N. Denzin & Y. Lincoln (Eds.), *The Sage handbook of qualitative research* (pp. 163–177). Los Angeles, CA: Sage.

Kitchen, J., & Stevens, D. (2005). Self-study in action research: Two teacher educators review their project and practice. *The Ontario Action Researcher, 8*(1). Retrieved from http://oar.nipissingu.ca/archive-V811E.htm

Kitchin, H. (2007). *Research ethics and the internet: Negotiating Canada's tri-council policy statement.* Black Point, Nova Scotia: Fernwood.

Knowles, J. G., & Cole, A. I. (2008). *Handbook of the arts in qualitative research: Perspectives, methodologies, examples, and issues.* Thousand Oaks, CA: Sage Publications.

Kovera, M. B. (2010). Confounding. In N. J. Salkind (Ed.), *Encyclopedia of research design* (pp. 220–222). Thousand Oaks, CA: Sage. doi:http://dx.doi.org/10.4135/9781412961288

Kozinets, R. (2015). Netnography. In R. Mansell & P. W. Ang (Eds.), *The international encyclopedia of digital communication and society.* Hoboken, NJ: John Wiley & Sons. doi:10.1002/9781118290743.wbiedsc067

Kramer, A., Guillory, J., & Hancock, J. (2014). Experimental evidence of massive-scale emotional contagion through social networks. *Proceedings of the National Academy of Sciences in the United States of America, 111*(24), 8788–8790. Retrieved from http://www.pnas.org/cgi/doi/10.1073/pnas.1320040111

Kraska, M. (2010). Quantitative research. In N. J. Salkind (Ed.), *Encyclopedia of research design* (pp. 1167–1172). Thousand Oaks, CA: Sage. doi:http://dx.doi.org/10.4135/9781412961288

Kvale, S. (1996). The 1000 page question. *Qualitative Inquiry, 2*(3), 275–284. doi:10.1177/107780049600200302

Lafrenière, D., & Cox, S. M. (2012). "If you can call it a poem": Toward a framework for the assessment of art-based works. *Qualitative Research, 13*(3), 318–336. doi:10.1177/1468794112446104

Lakkala, S. (2012). My doctoral thesis was about inclusion—emotions and technique. In K. Määttä (Ed.), *Obsessed with the doctoral thesis: Supervision and support during the thesis process* (pp. 13–16). Rotterdam: Sense Publishers.

Leavy, P. (2009). *Method meets art: Art-based research practice.* New York, NY: Guilford Press.

Leavy, P. (2013). *Fiction as research practice: Short stories, novellas, and novels*. Walnut Creek, CA: Left Coast Press.

Leavy, P. (2015). Introduction. In P. Leavy (Ed.), *The Oxford handbook of qualitative research* (pp. 1–13). New York, NY: Oxford University Press.

Lee, A. M. (2007). Developing effective supervisors: Concepts of research supervision. *South African Journal of Higher Education, 21*(4), 680–693.

Leech, N. L., & Onwuegbuzie, A. J. (2007). An array of qualitative data analysis tools: A call for data analysis triangulation. *School Psychology Quarterly, 22*(4), 557–584. doi:10.1037/1045-3830.22.4.557

Levin, M., & Greenwood, D. (2011). Revitalizing universities by reinventing the social sciences: Bildung and action research. In N. Denzin & Y. Lincoln (Eds.), *The Sage handbook of qualitative research* (pp. 27–42). Los Angeles, CA: Sage.

Lewin, K. (1946). Action research and minority problems. *Journal of Social Issues, 2*(4), 34–46. doi:10.1111/j.15404560.1946.tb02295.x

Lincoln, Y. S., & Guba, E. G. (1985). *Naturalistic inquiry*. Beverly Hills, CA: Sage.

Lincoln, Y. S., Lynham, S. A., & Guba, E. G. (2011). Paradigmatic controversies, contradictions, and emerging confluences. In N. Denzin & Y. Lincoln (Eds.), *The Sage handbook of qualitative research* (pp. 97–128). Los Angeles, CA: Sage.

Luttrell, W. (2000) "Good enough" methods for ethnographic research. *Harvard Educational Review, 70*(4), 499–524. doi:http://dx.doi.org/10.17763/haer.70.4.5333230502744141

MacDonald, C. (2012). Understanding participatory action research: A qualitative research methodology option. *Canadian Journal of Action Research, 13*(2), 34–50. Retrieved from http://cjar.nipissingu.ca/index.php/cjar/article/view/37

MacLeod, S. (2013). *Dans l'Griff-In Griffintown: Three personal French Canadian narratives on their homes, public spaces, and buildings in the former industrial neighbourhood of Griffintown* (Masters thesis). Concordia University, Québec. Retrieved from http://spectrum.library.concordia.ca/977057/

Machi, L., & McEnvoy, B. (2012). *The literature review: Six steps to success*. Thousand Oaks, CA: Corwin.

Malfroy, J. (2005). Doctoral supervision, workplace research and changing pedagogic practices. *Higher Education Research and Development, 24*(2), 165–178. doi:10.1080/07294360500062961

Manning, E. (2015). Against method. In P. Vannini (Ed.), *Non-representational methodologies: Re-envisioning research* (pp. 52–71). New York, NY: Routledge.

McAlpine, L., & Amundsen, C. (2011). Writing and speaking – learning the disciplinary language, talking the talk. In L. McAlpine & C. Amundsen (Eds.), *Doctoral education: Research-based strategies for doctoral students, supervisors and administrators* (pp. 57–58). Dordrecht: Springer.

McCallin, A., & Nayar, S. (2012). Postgraduate research supervision: A critical review of current practice. *Teaching in Higher Education, 17*(1), 63–74. Retrieved from http://dx.doi.org/10.1080/13562517.2011.590979

McNiff, J. (2013). *Action research: Principles and practices*. London & New York, NY: Routledge.

McNiff, S. (2008). Art-based research. In J. G. Knowles & A. I. Cole (Eds.), *Handbook of the arts in qualitative research: Perspectives, methodologies, examples, and issues* (pp. 29–40). Thousand Oaks, CA: Sage Publications.

Metcalfe, M. (2003). Author(ity): The literature review as expert witnesses. *Forum Qualitative Sozialforschung Forum: Qualitative Social Research, 4*(1), Art. 18. Retrieved from http://nbnresolving.de/urn:nbn:de:0114fqs0301187

Milech, B., & Schilo, A. (2009). 'Exit Jesus': Relating the exegesis and creative/production. *TEXT Special Issue, 3*. Retrieved from http://www.textjournal.com.au/speciss/issue3/ilechschilo.htm

Milkman, K., Akinola, M., & Chugh, D. (2013). Discrimination in the academy: A field experiment. *Social Science Research Network.* Retrieved from http://papers.ssrn.com/abstract=2063742

Moses, I. (1984). Supervision of higher degree students – Problem areas and possible solutions. *Higher Education Research & Development, 3*(2), 153–165. doi:10.1080/0729436840030204

Mullins, G., & Kiley, M. (2002). 'It's a PhD, not a Nobel Prize': How experienced examiners assess research theses. *Studies in Higher Education, 27*(4), 369–386. doi:10.1080/03075070220000011507

Mumby, D. (2012). *Graduate school: Winning strategies for getting in.* Rigaud, Québec: Pronto Press Publications.

Orb, A., Eisenhauer, L., & Wynaden, D. (2001). Ethics in qualitative research. *Journal of Nursing Scholarship, 33*(1), 93–96. doi:10.1111/j.1547-5069.2001.00093.x

Paltridge, B. (2002). Thesis and dissertation writing: An examination of published advice and actual practice. *English for Specific Purposes, 21*, 125–143. doi:10.1002/9781405198431.wbeal1211

Paré, A. (2011). Speaking of writing: Supervisory feedback and the dissertation. In L. McAlpine & C. Amundsen (Eds.), *Doctoral education: Research-based strategies for doctoral students, supervisors and administrators* (pp. 59–74). Dordrecht: Springer.

Park, C. (2003). In other (people's) words: plagiarism by university students-literature and lessons. *Assessment & Evaluation in Higher Education, 28*(5), 471–488. doi:10.1080/0260293032000120352

Pecorari, D. (2003). Good and original: Plagiarism and patchwriting in academic second-language writing. *Journal of Second Language Writing, 12*, 317–345. doi:10.1016/j.jslw.2003.08.004

Petticrew, M., Egan, M., Thomson, H., Hamilton, V., Kunkler, R., & Roberts, H. (2008). Publication bias in qualitative research: what becomes of qualitative research presented at conferences? *Journal of Epidemiology and Community Health, 62*(6), 552–554. Retrieved from http://dx.doi.org/10.1136/jech.2006.059394

Piirto, J. (2002). The question of quality and qualifications: writing inferior poems as qualitative research. *Qualitative Studies in Education, 15*(4), 431–445. doi:10.1080/09518390210145507

Purrington, C. (2014). *Designing conference posters.* Retrieved from http://colinpurrington.com/tips/academic/posterdesign

Randolf, J. (2009). A guide to writing the dissertation literature review. *Practical Assessment, Research & Evaluation, 14*(13), 1–13. Retrieved from http://pareonline.net/getvn.asp?v=14&n=13

Reilly, R. (2013). Me and Goldilocks…Searching for what is "just right" in trauma research: An autoethnography. *The Qualitative Report, 18*(93), 1–11. Retrieved from http://www.nova.edu/ssss/QR/QR18/reilly93.pdf

Riddett-Moore, K., & Siegesmund, R. (2012). Arts-based research: Data are constructed, not found. In S. Klein (Ed.), *Action research methods: Plain and simple* (pp. 105–132). New York, NY: Palgrave MacMillan.

Ridley, D. (2012). *The literature review: A step-by-step guide for students*. Los Angeles, CA: Sage.

Robinson-Cimpian, J. P. (2014). Inaccurate estimation of disparities due to mischievous responders: Several suggestions to assess conclusions. *Educational Researcher, 43*(4), 171–185.

Rolfe, G. (2006). Validity, trustworthiness and rigor: Quality and the idea of qualitative research. *Journal of Advanced Nursing, 53*(3), 304–310. Retrieved from http://www.ncbi.nlm.nih.gov/pubmed/16441535

Rothstein, H., Sutton, A., & Borenstein, M. (2005). Publication bias in meta-analysis. In H. Rothstein, A. Sutton, & M. Borenstein (Eds.), *Publication bias in meta-analysis – Prevention, assessment and adjustments* (pp. 1–7). West Sussex, England: John Wiley & Sons, Ltd.

Sage. (n.d.). *How to get your journal article published*. Retrieved from www.sagepub.com/upmdata/63382_how_to_get_published.pdf

Sakulku, J., & Alexander, J. (2011). The imposter phenomenon. *International Journal of Behavioral Science, 6*(1), 73–92. Retrieved from http://www.tcithaijo.org/index.php/IJBS/article/view/521/pdf

Saldaña, J. (2013). *Coding manual for qualitative researchers*. Thousand Oaks, CA: Sage.

Sandelowski, M. (1993). Rigor or rigor mortis: The problem of rigor in qualitative research revisited. *Advanced Nursing Science, 16*(2), 1–8. Retrieved from http://www.ncbi.nlm.nih.gov/pubmed/8311428

Saunders, B., Kitzinger, J., & Kitzinger, C. (2014). Anonymising interview data: Challenges and compromise in practice. *Qualitative Research, 17*(5), 616–632. doi:10.1177/1468794114550439

Sheltzer, J., & Smith, J. (2014). Elite male faculty in life science employ fewer women. *Proceedings of the National Academy of Sciences in the United States of America, 111*(28), 10107–10112. Retrieved from www.pnas.org/cgi/doi/10.1073/pnas.1403334111

Silva, P. J. (2007). *How to write a lot: A practical guide to productive academic writing*. Washington, DC: American Psychological Association.

Silver, C., & Lewins, A. F. (2015). Computer-assisted analysis of qualitative data. In P. Leavy (Ed.), *The Oxford handbook of qualitative research* (pp. 606–638) New York, NY: Oxford University Press.

Simons, H. (2015). Case study research: In-depth understanding in context. In P. Leavy (Ed.), *The Oxford handbook of qualitative research* (pp. 1–13) New York, NY: Oxford University Press.

Single, P. B. (2010). *Demystifying dissertation writing: A streamlined process from choice of topic to final text*. Virginia, VA: Stylus.

Smeby, J.-C. (2000). Same-gender relationships in graduate supervision. *Higher Education, 40*(1), 53–67. Retrieved from http://dx.doi.org/10.1023/A:1004040911469

Snow, S., Snow, S., & D'Amico, M. (2008). Interdisciplinary research through community music therapy and performance ethnography/Recherche Interdisciplinaire: Musicothérapie communautaire et ethnographie de la performance. *Canadian Journal of Music Therapy, 14*(1), 30–46. Retrieved from https://www.questia.com/read/1P31647756391/interdisciplinary-research-through-community-music

Spaulding, L., & Rockinson-Szapkiw, A. (2012). Hearing their voices: Factors doctoral candidates attribute to their persistence. *International Journal of Doctoral Studies, 7*, 199–219. Retrieved from http://ijds.org/Volume7/IJDSv7p199-219Spaulding334.pdf

Spencer, R., Pryce, J. M., & Walsh, J. (2015). Philosophical approaches to qualitative research. In P. Leavy (Ed.), *The Oxford handbook of qualitative research* (pp. 1–13). New York, NY: Oxford University Press.

Starke-Meyerring, D. (2011). The paradox of writing in doctoral education: Student experiences. In L. McAlpine & C. Amundsen (Eds.), *Doctoral education: Research-based strategies for doctoral students, supervisors and administrators* (pp. 75–95). Dordrecht: Springer.

Starks, H., & Trinidad, H. B. (2007). Choose your method: A comparison between phenomenology, discourse analysis, and grounded theory. *Qualitative Health Research, 17*(10), 1372–1380. Retrieved from http://www.ncbi.nlm.nih.gov/pubmed/18000076

Streiner, D. L., & Sidani, S. (2010). *When research goes off the rails: Why it happens and what you can do about it.* New York, NY: Guiford Press.

Sturken, M., & Cartwright, L. (2001). *Practices of looking: An introduction to visual culture.* New York, NY: Oxford University Press.

Sutherland-Smith, W. (2005). Pandora's box: Academic perceptions of student plagiarism in writing. *Journal of English for Academic Purposes, 4*, 83–95. doi:10.1016/j.jeap.2004.07.007

Tedlock, B. (2011). Braiding narrative ethnography with memoir and creative non-fiction. In N. Denzin & Y. Lincoln (Eds.), *The Sage handbook of qualitative research* (pp. 331–340). Los Angeles, CA: Sage.

Tenenbaum, H., Crosby, F., & Gliner, M. (2001). Mentoring relationships in graduate school. *Journal of Vocational Behavior, 59*, 326–341. Retrieved from http://dx.doi.org/10.1006/jvbe.2001.1804

Tolich, M. (2010). A critique of current practice: Ten foundational guidelines for autoethnographers. *Qualitative Health Research, 20*(12), 1599–1610. doi:10/1177/1049732310376076

Trent, A., & Cho, J. (2015). Interpreting strategies: Appropriate concepts. In P. Leavy (Ed.), *The Oxford handbook of qualitative research* (pp. 639–657). New York, NY: Oxford University Press.

Trobia, A. (2008). Questionnaire. In P. Lavrakas (Ed.), *Encyclopedia of survey research methods* (pp. 652–644). Thousand Oaks, CA: Sage. doi:http://dx.doi.org/10.4135/9781412963947

United States Department of Health and Human Services. (2009). *Protection of human subjects.* Retrieved from http://www.hhs.gov/ohrp/humansubjects/guidance/45cfr46.html

University of Toronto School of Graduate Studies. (2007). *Intellectual property guidelines for graduate students & supervisors.* Retrieved from http://www.sgs.utoronto.ca/currentstudents/Pages/Intellectual-Property-Guidelines.aspx

Urquhart, C. (2013). *Grounded theory for qualitative research: A practical guide.* Thousand Oaks, CA: Sage.

van Manen, M. (1997). *Researching lived experience: Human science for an action sensitive pedagogy.* London: The Althouse Press.

Vaughan, K. (2005). Pieced together: Collage as an artist's method for interdisciplinary research. *International Journal of Qualitative Methods, 4*(1), 1–21. Retrieved from https://www.ualberta.ca/~iiqm/backissues/4_1/html/vaughan.htm

Verma, I. (2014). Editorial expression of concern and correction. *Proceedings of the National Academy of Sciences in the United States of America, 111*(29), 10779. Retrieved from http://www.pnas.org/cgi/doi/10.1073/pnas.1412469111

Vigen, T. (2015). *Spurious correlations*. New York, NY: Hyperion.

Walsh, D., & Downe. (2005). Meta-synthesis method for qualitative research: A literature review. *Methodological Issues in Nursing Research, 50*(2), 204–211. doi:10.1111/j.1365-2648.2005.03380.x

Wellington, J. (2010). Supporting students' preparation for the viva: Their preconceptions and implications for practice. *Teaching in Higher Education, 15*(1), 71–84. doi:10.1080/13562510903487867.

Wellington, J., & Sikes, P. (2006). A doctorate in a tight compartment: why do students choose a professional doctorate and what impact does it have on their professional lives? *Studies in Higher Education, 31*(6), 723–734. Retrieved from http://dx.doi.org/10.1080/03075070601004358

Wenger, E. (1999). *Communities of practice: Learning, meaning, and identity*. Cambridge: Cambridge University Press.

Wheeldon, J., & Ahlberg, M. K. (2012). *Visualizing social science research: Maps, methods, & meaning*. Thousand Oaks, CA: Sage.

Wiles, R. (2013). *What are qualitative research ethics?* London: Bloomsbury.

Wilhite, A., & Fong, E. (2012). Coercive citation in academic publishing. *Science, 335*, 542–543. doi:10.1126/science.1212540

Yin, R. K. (2009). *Case study research design and methods*. Thousand Oaks, CA: Sage.

Zhou, Y., Jindal-Snape, D., Topping, K., & Todman, J. (2008). Theoretical models of culture shock and adaption in international students in higher education. *Studies in Higher Education, 33*(1), 63–75. Retrieved from http://dx.doi.org/10/1080/03075070701794833

Zimmer, L. (2006). Qualitative meta-synthesis: A question of dialoguing with the texts. *Journal of Advanced Nursing, 53*(3), 311–318. doi:10.1111/j.1365-2648.2006.03721.x

ABOUT THE AUTHOR

Lorrie Blair is a Professor of Art Education at Concordia University in Montréal, Québec. With over 25 years post-secondary teaching experience, she has held positions at universities in the United States and Canada. She is active as a supervisor of MA and Ph.D. thesis students and was a recent recipient of the Faculty of Fine Arts Distinguished Teaching Award.

Dr. Blair's teaching and research interests include teacher identity, teenage cultural practices, qualitative and arts methodologies, and exploring effective, interdisciplinary, and sustainable design in teacher education at the post-secondary level. She has published nationally and internationally and has given numerous conference presentations and in-service sessions in these areas. Her research has been funded by the Social Science and Humanities Research Council's Workshop and Insight Grants and the *Fonds pour la formation de chercheurs et l'aide à la recherche*.

Dr. Blair's has held administrative posts including graduate program director, department chair, and an associate dean of students. She is a Fellow of the School of Canadian Irish Studies and Concordia's School of Graduate Studies.

Printed in the United States
By Bookmasters